ERAS OF NONCONFORMITY.

Edited by
REV. C. SILVESTER HORNE, M.A.

A Series of volumes, embracing the complete history of the Free Churches of Britain. Size foolscap 8vo, uniformly bound in cloth, gilt, price 1s. each net.

London : National Council of the Evangelical Free Churches, Thomas Law, Memorial Hall, E.C.

V

THE RISE OF THE QUAKERS

GEORGE FOX.

From the original painting by Sir Peter Lely in the Friends' Historical Library of Swarthmore College, Pennsylvania. Reproduced by kind permission.

THE RISE
OF THE QUAKERS

BY

T. EDMUND HARVEY

NATIONAL COUNCIL OF EVANGELICAL FREE CHURCHES
London : Thomas Law, Memorial Hall, E.C.

HEADLEY BROTHERS, 14, BISHOPSGATE STREET WITHOUT, E.C.
MCMIX

Fifth Impression, corrected.

CONTENTS

The original spelling of the quotations has been usually modernised, and in one case a grammatical correction has been made.

T. E. H.

I

INTRODUCTORY

THE rise of the Society of Friends is so closely bound up with the story of the life of George Fox that it is hardly possible to write of one without treating of the other. And yet no one would have been prompter than George Fox himself to disclaim the position which we might so naturally give him as founder of the Society of Friends. For, indeed, the history of the early Quakers is not that of a man, but of a movement. Before Fox began to preach men were feeling after the truths which he proclaimed ; not only were doctrines afterwards distinctive of Quakerism held here and there by one and another of the many religious bodies which perplex the ecclesiastical historian of the seventeenth century, but up and down England little companies of "Seekers," as they called themselves, were accustomed to meet together to search after fuller knowledge of the truth, and often

to wait in silence before God in faith that He
would teach them, though all the preachers
of the different Churches without had failed
to do so. Thus in the brief narrative of
the spreading of truth inserted by George
Fox in his Journal for the year 1676[1] he is
able to speak of the gathering together of
Friends as a people in Leicestershire as early
as 1644, though his own work as a preacher
is not usually accounted to have begun till
1647. In his Journal for this period he speaks
of talking with "friendly people" who would
doubtless be Seekers or in sympathy with
them—men and women weary of the for-
malism of the Puritans, tired of the endless
theological subtleties of so many of their
preachers, longing in their hearts for a religion which should touch not only their
intellects, but their inmost souls.

It is difficult for us to-day to picture the
conditions of life in England when George
Fox began his great work. But we may feel
something of the difference from our own
time in reading John Bunyan's story of his
own life in "Grace Abounding." One is
struck with the way in which the paramount
interest of everyday men and women lies in
religion : poor women in the street talk about

[1] Journal, vol. ii. p. 251.

sin and salvation; the simple Bedfordshire tinker is haunted by the horror of his own wickedness and the dread of hell, and the innocent art of bell-ringing becomes to him the subtlest snare of the Evil One. The religious experiences of Fox and Bunyan only show more clearly and in greater measure what a thousand other souls about them were passing through and striving after. Everywhere men were endeavouring to arrive at better forms of worship and Church government, aiming at lives purer from ill, secretly longing for a deeper and more living faith. The great majority of the band of Quaker preachers who, within a few years of the time when Fox began his public ministry, went about the country in the same service of truth, had passed through many phases of belief before they found rest and a new life in the gospel of the universal and saving Light.

It is noteworthy, too, that the men who were the instruments of this great religious movement were in most cases far below the opponents against whom they found themselves pitted, in intellectual equipment as well as social position. Despite the keen ability to seize an advantage of argument and the strong mother-wit which George Fox's Journal so often reveals, the victories of the early Quakers were not won by force of argument. Their constant appeal was to the witness of God in the souls of their hearers, and their endeavour was to arouse that in the listeners' hearts which would in time bring convincement to them. And sometimes it was a power beyond the expression of words which made itself felt on those who came into contact with them, and kindled a like response within them. None, perhaps, have written more beautifully of this than Robert Barclay, the scholar trained in the Scottish Jesuit College at Paris, who, as he tells us, " not by strength of arguments or by a particular disquisition of each doctrine and convincement of my understanding thereby, came to receive and bear witness of the truth ; but by being secretly reached by this life. For when," he goes on, " I came into the silent assemblies of God's people, I felt a secret power among them which touched my heart ; and as I gave way unto it, I found the evil weakening in me, and the good raised up ; and so I became thus knit and united to them, hungering more and more after the increase of this power and life whereby I might feel myself perfectly redeemed.[1]

[1] Barclay, *Apology*, Proposition xi., "Of Worship."

Such was the convincement the early Quakers sought to bring about. Illustrating this from another standpoint, George Whitehead's autobiography gives a vivid picture of the effect produced on his mind when, as a thoughtful young man in search for some better food than the Presbyterians had been able to give him, he first attended a meeting of the Quakers at Sunny Bank, near Grayrigg, in Westmoreland.

" At my first going to the said Meeting, what was most observable to me was when I came into the said Meeting and sate down seriously among them, after a little space of silence, a Friend (one Thomas Arey) spoke a little while of the spiritual deliverance, travels and progress of the Lord's people in His way and work; alluding to Israel's deliverance out of Egypt, from under Pharaoh and his task-masters, &c. . . . All which I thought I easily understood allegorically, or mysteriously, as spiritualised ; but there appeared to me a great work of the power of the Lord in the Meeting, breaking of the hearts of divers into great sorrow, weeping and contrition of spirit, which I believe was a godly sorrow for sin, in order to unfeigned repentance.

" I was the more confirmed herein, seeing a young maid go mourning out of the Meeting, whom I seriously followed to observe her sorrowful condition, and beholding her being sate down on the ground, with her face down toward the earth, as if she regarded nobody present, she, mourning bitterly, cried out, 'Lord, make me clean; O Lord, make me clean.' Which did far more tenderly and deeply affect my heart than what I had heard spoken, and more than all the preaching that ever I had heard from man or men; and was a certain testimony to me, the Spirit of the Lord evidencing to my spirit that it was a real work of His power upon her heart." [1]

This experience of George Whitehead's may well represent to us the way in which the Quaker movement grew. It was not by eloquence of preaching, and often in spite of lack of all the accustomed training of learned study and of practical experience, that this new evangel spread through village and town, from yeomen's farms and country cottages, from merchants' houses and tradesmen's shops, where there assembled together the little groups of men and women, known to each other as the " Friends of Truth " and to those about them as " Quakers." As in the days of the early Church, these gatherings of believers were for the most part held in private houses,

[1] G. Whitehead, *Christian Progress*, pt. i. p.3.

and were far more numerous than at first sight appears. We have no means of judging the numbers of such meetings in the earliest days, but the records of Quarter Sessions show that when under the Toleration Act of 1690 a licence was taken out for such meetings, there were nearly 400 held in Yorkshire alone, many of them in places in which to-day one would not otherwise have known that there had ever been any Quakers. That the ideal Friends' Meeting was felt to be a small rather than a large gathering was shown by the arrangements made in the early days in London by which a number of more or less private meetings were held in Friends' houses attended by those already convinced of the truth of the new views; while Edward Burrough and his fellow-ministers went to the great public meetings in Gracechurch Street or at the " Bull and Mouth," where they were prepared to find an unruly multitude of scoffers, mingled with others more seriously inclined—meetings in which their work was that of threshing out the good wheat from the chaff, and sending on in due time one after another to join the quiet meetings held in private houses. But one can hardly do justice to the history of the early Quakers by plunging thus into the midst of the subject ; and though one needs to realise something of the religious atmosphere that surrounded the movement and made it what it was, it is natural that in telling the story of its rise we should turn to the life of Fox himself.

THE EARLY LIFE OF GEORGE FOX

THERE seems to have been little in the family surroundings and early education of George Fox to mark him out from his fellows. He was born in 1624, at Fenny Drayton, in Leicestershire, of simple middle-class parents. His father, Christopher Fox—"righteous Christer," as the neighbours called him—was a weaver by trade, and apparently in sufficiently easy circumstances to allow of his proposing to bring up the quiet, earnest-minded lad with a view to his being ordained in the Church of England; but other counsels prevailed, and he was apprenticed instead to a shoe-maker and grazier. George Fox makes but the briefest mention of his father in his Journal, which was written rather as a spiritual history than as a biographical record. We do, however, get one little picture of him

1624

at a later date, standing with his cane in his hand listening to a dispute between the rector, Nathaniel Stephens, and his son, and in spite of his having sided with his parson (whose churchwarden he once had been), recognising that the victory lay with George, and crying out as he struck his cane upon the ground, "Truly I see, he that will but stand to the truth, it will carry him out." [1] Christopher Fox never seems to have become a Quaker, but, as his son wrote, "he was an honest man, and there was a seed of God in him." His mother would seem to have had a deeper influence upon Fox. Mary Lago was, as Penn tells us, "a woman accomplished above most of her degree in the place where she lived," [2] and was "tender and indulgent" to her son's serious ways, by which he was marked out from his other brothers and sisters. She came, as Fox tells us, "of the stock of the martyrs," and more than one reference which he makes in his writings to the heroes of the persecution in Queen Mary's time shows how deep the impress of their battle for the truth must have been upon his mind. Doubtless he would often hear as a child his mother tell

[1] Journal, i. 206 (8th edition, 2 vols. 1891. 8vo.).
[2] Penn's Preface to George Fox's Journal, p. xliv.

of the trials of those dark days, and of how
her relations had suffered. He would hear
of Robert Glover's firm endurance, even when
for days before his martyrdom no assurance
of Divine support was given him, until at
last, as he walked to the stake, he felt about
him the Presence for which he longed,
and cried joyfully to his friend, "Austen,
He is come! He is come!" and the
long trials of the brothers John and
William Glover—John hunted by the officers and spending nights in hiding in the
wet woods ; William driven from his native
town to die in a Shropshire village ; the
bodies of both cast forth from churchyard
and church and buried with ignominy as
damned heretics. The soul of the lad would
be stirred within him as he listened, and
perhaps in later days the memory of his fore-
fathers and their struggle would nerve him
for the persecution he too had to face.[1]

The influence of home and Church were
alike Puritan in tendency. Nathaniel Stephens,
who was appointed to the living in 1640,
became a Presbyterian under the Long Parliament, and was ultimately ejected for non-
conformity after the Restoration. There

[1] See Foxe, *Acts and Monuments*, and Richings,
The Mancetter Martyrs, 1860 ; cf. *Dict. Nat. Biography*, article on Fox.

seems to be nothing to show that George Fox
ever came into contact in his earlier years
with any of the school of Laud and Andrewes,
and though as a child he would, no doubt, be
familiar with the liturgy of the Prayer Book,
the atmosphere in which he grew up was that
of the Puritan Church of the Civil War, and
the Quaker movement was hardly influenced
at all directly by the teaching of the Anglican
Church. When, in 1665, George Fox lay in
prison in Scarborough Castle, Dr. Cradock,
one of the clergy who came to dispute with
him, was frankly taxed by the Quaker leader
with his inconsistency in excommunicating
a number of Friends, "for not coming to
church," as the clergyman said. "Why, ye
left us above twenty years ago, when we were
but young lads and lasses, to the Presbyterians, Independents, and Baptists, many of
whom made spoil of our goods and persecuted us because we would not follow them.
Now we, being but young, knew little then of
your principles, and if ye had intended to
keep the old men that did know them to
you, and your principles alive, that we might
have known them, ye should either not have
fled from us as ye did, or ye should have sent
us your epistles, collects, homilies, and evening songs, for Paul wrote epistles to the

saints though he was in prison. But they
and we might have turned Turks or Jews for
any collects, homilies, or epistles we had from
you all this while. And now thou hast ex-
communicated us, both young and old, and
so have others of you done : that is, ye have
put us out of your Church, before ye have
got us into it."[1]

"When I came to eleven years of age,"
writes Fox, "I knew pureness and righteousness, for while a child I was taught how to
walk to be kept pure,"[2] and while he served
his master his truthfulness of speech became
a proverb to his neighbours. "If George says
Verily, there is no altering him." Though it
is possible that he worked enough with his
master to be able a little later to make himself[3] that famous suit of leather in which he
went on his journeys, and of which Carlyle
has so well written, it was chiefly in tending
the sheep that his time was employed. And

[1] Journal, ii. 64.
[2] Journal, i. 2 ; and Penn, Preface, p. liv.
[3] There seems to be no evidence for Fox having
made the suit himself. Sewell says he wore it not on
account of his former trade, but for convenience in
travel, to avoid constant repairs to his clothes.
Croese tells of his being known on account of it as
'the Leather Man."

here in the open air, alone with the flocks, he must often have pondered over the problems of life and religion, and sought after some better solution than his rector was able to give him. The turning-point of his life came, as it has so often done to others, in a seemingly trifling incident. It was in the summer of 1643 that he had been on business to a fair, and was asked by a cousin to join him and a friend, both of them " professors "—Puritans making profession of their religion—in drinking a jug of beer. George was thirsty, and accepted the invitation, the more readily, as he tells us, because he " loved any that had a sense of good, or that sought after the Lord." After each had drunk a glass, the others began drinking healths, calling for more, and agreeing that he who would not drink should pay for all. Telling the story in his Journal, Fox writes : " I was grieved that any who made profession of religion should do so. They grieved me very much, having never had such a thing put to me before by any sort of people ; wherefore I rose up to go, and putting my hand into my pocket, laid a groat on the table before them, and said, ' If it be so, I will leave you.' "[1]

1643

[1] Journal, i. 3.

When he reached home he did not go to bed that night, but walked to and fro, or knelt in prayer, pouring out the trouble of his heart to God.

Common enough it must have been then, as now, to see men drinking themselves drunk in the taverns "for good-fellowship's sake"; what had so touched him must have been the sudden shock of the contrast between the outward appearance and the inward reality. In an instant of time had been made clear to him the sham of this formal religion these men professed; the starched mask of Puritanism fell for a moment and revealed beneath it the features of an evil nature, the passions of earth, concealed, but unsubdued. George Fox realised that religion must go to the roots of being or it was no religion at all. This religion his friends professed was a sham, a failure; and now he felt the voice of God calling him to leave all, young and old alike, and go forth as a stranger in quest of the Divine Truth.

"Then," he goes on, "at the command of God, on the ninth day of the seventh month, 1643, I left my relations and broke off all familiarity of fellowship with old or young,"[1] and he set out on his travels, journeying from

[1] Journal, i. 3.

place to place, seeking, but not finding, and
sometimes almost in despair.

Troubled at length lest he should grieve
his relatives by his absence, he returned from
London to Leicestershire. Some of his relations wished him to marry, and others would
have him enlist in the army; no one seemed
in any way to understand his trouble; sometimes the rector would converse with him
and encourage him; " Never was such a
plant bred in England," he once exclaimed.[1]

But when Stephens began to preach on the
young man's talks with him in his sermons in
church on Sunday, Fox was not pleased, and
he soon turned to other places in hopes of
finding better teachers. One tried to cure
him with physic; another lost his temper
when he trod on a flower-bed; a third kindly
old clergyman bade him " take tobacco and

[1] Calamy's account of Stephens is of considerable
interest, and gives an attractive picture of him in his
old age as an ejected Nonconformist. "The noted
Quaker, George Fox, came out of his little parish.
Mr. Stephens had much discourse with him, but with
little effect. He thought his time better spent in
instructing a teachable people; which he did very
diligently. He took much pains in studying the
book of the Revelation; and some apprehended that
few ever did it to better purpose" (Calamy, *Non-
conformists' Memorial*, vol. ii., ed. 1802).

sing psalms!" "When the time called Christmas came," he writes, "while others were feasting and sporting themselves, I looked out poor widows from house to house, and gave them some money. When I was invited to marriages (as I sometimes was) I went to none at all, but the next day, or soon after, I would go and visit them, and if they were poor, I gave them some money; for I had wherewith both to keep myself from being chargeable to others, and to administer something to the necessities of those who were in need."[1]

At this time the clouds about him lifted; as he was nearing Coventry in 1646, ponder-

1646 ing the saying that "all Christians are believers, both Protestants and Papists," there came to him the message that to be a Christian meant passing from death to life, and that such alone were in reality believers who had gone through this birth into the true life. A little later another message showed him that "to be bred at Oxford or Cambridge was not enough to fit and qualify men to be ministers of Christ," at which, he tells us, he wondered, "seeing that it was the common belief of people." Meanwhile his friends were troubled that he

[1] Journal, i. 7.

3

preferred to go into an orchard with his Bible
alone rather than to hear the clergyman with
them in church.

He was already coming to see beyond the
ideas in which he had grown up with regard
to the holiness of any sacred building. " It
was opened to me," he writes, "that God,
who made the world, did not dwell in temples
made with hands, and this seemed at first a
strange word, because both priests and people
used to call their temples or churches dreadful
places, holy ground, and the temple of God.
But the Lord showed me clearly that He did
not dwell in these temples which men had
commanded and set up, but in people's
hearts." [1]   Yet these moments of vision alter-
nated with times of great trouble and temptation. " I fasted much," Fox writes, "and
walked abroad in solitary places many days,
and often took my Bible and went and sat in
hollow trees and lonesome places till night
came on, and frequently in the night walked
mournfully abroad by myself, for I was a
man of sorrows in the times of the first
workings of the Lord in me." [2]

He had already given up hope of effectual
help from the clergy of the National Church,
and now he found that none of the preachers

[1] Journal, i. 8.   [2] i. 10.

of the various sects he came across were able to supply what he needed. And at length, he tells us, "when all my hopes in them and in all men were gone, so that I had nothing outwardly to help me, nor could I tell what to do, then, O! then I heard a voice which said, 'There is one, even Christ Jesus, that can speak to thy condition,' and when I heard it my heart did leap for joy." What he had sought in vain from men he found in the depths of his own heart, in the inward presence of the Spirit of Christ, enlightening his darkness and leading him along the way of truth.

Now the meaning of the truths of the Scriptures began to come home to him as never before; a new hope had entered into his life and a new strength in temptation; "a secret anchor"[1] realised as holding him fast, even when unseen amid the waves. He tells us how at one time he was "wrapped up in the love of God, so that I could not but admire the greatness of His love," and realised that all his troubles and temptations were for his good; that "that which could not abide in the patience nor endure the fire, in the light I found it to be the groans of the flesh, that could not give up to the will of

Journal, i. 14.

God, which had veiled me ; and that could
not be patient in all trials, troubles, and
perplexities, could not give up self to die
by the Cross, the power of God. . . ." With
the realisation of the two natures at war in
the soul of man came also the knowledge of
the liberty that comes with the daily cruci-
fixion of the lower self—"If ye join to the
Spirit and serve God in it, ye have liberty
and victory over the flesh and its works.
Therefore keep in the daily cross the power
of God, by which you may witness all that
to be crucified which is contrary to the will
of God, and which shall not come into His
kingdom." [1]

The great truth of this experience brought
Fox for the first time into open conflict with
the religious people amongst whom
he was travelling. In the earlier
part of 1647 he had travelled through parts
of Derbyshire and Nottinghamshire and
found sympathetic spirits, amongst whom he
names Elizabeth Hooton, who, at a little
later date, was the first woman to travel
about as a Quaker minister.

1647

Now he came to Lancashire and found an
audience amongst the Puritans of Manchester.
"Some were convinced," he writes, "who

[1] Journal, i. 18.

received the Lord's teaching, by which they were confirmed and stood in the truth. But the professors were in a rage, all pleading for sin and imperfection, and could not endure to hear talk of perfection and of a holy and sinless life." [1]

We have here the first mention of a controversy which went on throughout the century between the Quakers and their Puritan opponents, one which was taken up again by other writers when the Methodists championed the same cause.

The teaching of Fox on Christian perfection is intimately associated with his own spiritual experience. He had been revolted by the unreality of a religion which did not affect the whole moral life of its professors, and to him the humility of the Puritan divines, who maintained that man must always be sinful, meant the abandonment of the victorious struggle against evil which was the outcome of obedience to the spirit and life of Christ ; it opened the door to hypocrisy and self-indulgence and made the Gospel of none effect.

He could not rest content with the legalist's notion of a remission of the penalties of sin while the evil itself remained uncured.

[1] Journal, i. 19.

Christianity meant to him a renewal of the whole nature, the healing of the disease of the soul, and not merely freedom from its painful consequences. This does not mean that he ever taught that there was not to be a "daily warfare" against evil, but it was against evil recognised as outside of our true nature.

Nor did this perfection mean attaining a level above which one could not rise ; it rather involved and implied continual growth —indeed, "growth in the truth" was a constant watchword with the early Friends. And, finally, George Fox was most insistent in his endeavours to show that this teaching did not lead those who followed it into spiritual pride, but necessarily involved just the reverse. "We are nothing, Christ is all," was his reply to one who had endeavoured to ensnare him into some declaration of his own righteousness. The Christian has no life or goodness apart from the one source of all life and virtue, and the victory he wins is not his own, but that of the power of the Divine Spirit working in him. As we look back upon this great controversy we may perhaps feel that there was truth on both sides ; each was trying to emphasise an essential part of our nature, without which the moral life would not exist; and yet we may feel that the higher truth was grasped by the Quaker and Methodist preachers. If it be true that our evil nature is always with us, the body, with all its cravings, inherited and acquired, memory and imagination, with all their tendencies to drag us down and lead astray, yet only as we realise that it is not here that our life consists, and that this is not our true self, does the victory over evil become possible. To the Christian the mainspring of life, the source of all power, is in that other life which is not his, but God's; and as he realises that the life of God is present in the soul of man, and submits his will wholly to it, the new nature, the true self, is built up in him. The struggle goes on, the lower self dies slowly, and we may come at length to recognise as evil what once we thought of as harmless; but to tolerate the existence of evil in our lives alongside of good is to make a truce which must stop all moral growth. The evil only exists to be driven out and overcome.

Thus began the long public ministry of George Fox, now, as for so many years, rousing the bitterest antagonism amongst a large number of the ministers and church-goers with whom he came into contact, and yet always appealing to other listeners who

seemed waiting for just such a message;
often also reaching beyond the arguments
raised against it to the very depths of his
opponents' hearts, arousing in them that
inward witness to which he made appeal,
so that in spite of themselves they were won
over to confess the truth.

But Fox had yet to pass through a period
of doubt and difficulty. He went back to
Nottinghamshire, and there, he
1647 tells us, "the Lord showed me that
the natures of those things which were hurtful without were within, in the hearts and
minds of wicked men." Troubled with the
sense of this evil, he cried to the Lord saying,
"'Why should I be thus, seeing I was never
addicted to commit those evils?' and the
Lord answered 'That it was needful I should
have a sense of all conditions, how else
should I speak to all conditions!' and in
this I saw the infinite Love of God. I saw
also that there was an ocean of darkness
and death; but an infinite ocean of light
and love which flowed over the ocean of
darkness." [1]

People began to come from a distance to
see "the young man that had a discerning
spirit," and his words were listened to with

[1] Journal, i. 19, 20; i. 24.

eager interest. Fox, too, would go to meetings
that the Puritans held in various places in
the neighbourhood and take part in discussion or in prayer, though when he was asked
to pray again that the deep impression a
former prayer of his had made might be
renewed, he tells us how "he could not pray
in man's will." He spoke to one company
of how the blood of Christ of which they
were discoursing must be sought in the
heart and conscience, and to another
gathering at Leicester of the true meaning of
the Church as a spiritual household of which
Christ was the head; on both occasions he
had to meet considerable opposition.

A little later he passed into the Vale of
Beavor, preaching as he went. And here
one morning, he tells us, "as I was sitting by
the fire, a great cloud came over me, and a
temptation beset me; but I sat still. And
it was said, 'All things come by nature;'
and the elements and stars came over me, so
that I was in a manner quite clouded with it.
But as I sat still and silent, the people of the
house perceived nothing. And as I sat still
under it, and let it alone, a living hope arose
in me, and a true voice, which said, 'There *is*
a living God who made all things.' And
immediately the cloud and temptation

vanished away and life rose over it all; my
heart was glad, and I praised the living God.
After some time, I met with some people
who had a notion that there was no God, but
that all things come by nature. I had a
great dispute with them, and overturned
them, and made some of them confess that
there is a living God, and then I saw that it
was good that I had gone through that
exercise." [1] How many preachers before and
after George Fox had failed to touch their
hearers because they lacked just this inward
understanding of and sympathy with the
condition of those to whom he spoke, of
which we get a glimpse in this passage. In
this case he not only saw the condition in
which the men stood, but had himself gone
through something of the experience, and he
perceives that he could not have given the
true answer to doubt had he not known
himself what doubt meant.

And now people friendly to his teaching
were beginning to meet together regularly in
more places than one. He speaks
1648   in his Journal for the year 1648
of there being a Meeting of Friends at Eaton,
near Derby, the first occasion on which the
term afterwards adopted by the new Society
is used by Fox.

[1] Journal, i. 26.

In the midst of such work as this it is characteristic of Fox that he felt it his duty to go and speak a message to the Justices who were at the time sitting in connection with one of the periodic hirings of servants, to warn them not to oppress the servants in their wages. Again and again in his Journal [1] we find record of this eagerness of his to apply the principles of Christianity to all the social relationships of men, and to expose the worthlessness of a religion which did not concern itself with removing injustice and impurity from the lives of its followers.

In all this he felt the profound gulf that lay between the professed aim of clergy, physicians, and lawyers, and their actual lives and practice. And now, he tells us, " the Lord God opened to me by His invisible power that every man was enlightened by the Divine light of Christ ; and I saw it shine through all ; and that they that believed in it came out of condemnation to the light of life and became the children of it ; but they that hated it, and did not believe in it, were condemned by it, though they made a profession of Christ. This I saw in the pure openings of the light, without the help of any man ; neither did I then know where to find

[1] Journal, i. 34–35.

it in the Scriptures, though afterwards, searching the Scriptures, I found it. For I saw in that Light and Spirit which was before the Scriptures were given forth, and which led the holy men of God to give them forth, that all must come to that Spirit if they would know God or Christ or the Scriptures aright, which they that gave them forth were led and taught by." [1]

With this message burning in his heart Fox went forth. "With and by this Divine power and Spirit of God, and the light of Jesus, I was to bring people off from all their own ways, to Christ, the new and living Way; and from their churches which men had made and gathered, to the Church in God, the general assembly written in heaven which Christ is the head of: and off from the world's teachers, made by men, to learn of Christ . . . and off from all the world's worships, to know the Spirit of Truth in the inward parts, and to be led thereby; that in it they might worship the Father of Spirits. . . . And I was to bring people off from all the world's religions, which are vain, that they might know the pure religion, might visit the fatherless, the widows, and the strangers, and keep themselves from the spots

[1] Journal, i. 34.

of the world; then there would not be so
many beggars, the sight of whom often
grieved my heart, as it denoted so much hard-
heartedness amongst them that professed the
name of Christ. . ."

"When the Lord sent me forth into the
world," Fox goes on, " He forbade me to put
off my hat to any, high or low; and I was
required to Thee and Thou all men and
women, without any respect to rich or poor,
great or small. . . . Neither might I bow
or scrape with my leg to any one; and this
made the sects and professions to rage." [1]

It is difficult for us to-day to realise the
bitter suffering which this step involved for
George Fox and his friends; nor perhaps at
first sight is it easy to realise how much was
implied in their protest.

In doing what they did they were not
merely shocking the conventions of the day,
but making an appeal from a pagan class
system masquerading under the guise of
Christianity to the deep underlying principles
of the social teaching of Jesus, involving the
recognition of human brotherhood in the
realities of life as well as in the formulæ of
worship.

The storm of opposition aroused by this

[1] Journal, i. 38.

fearless stand made by the early Quakers for
manhood and fraternity shows that their
opponents felt that this was no mere quib-
bling of grammatical precisians. "O! the
blows, punchings, beatings, and imprisonments that we underwent, for not putting off
our hats to men! . . . The bad language
and evil usage we received on this account are
hard to be expressed, besides the danger we
were sometimes in, of losing our lives for this
matter, and that by the great professors of
Christianity, who thereby evinced that they
were not true believers."

Fox passed about upon his errand pleading
in the law courts for a truer spirit of justice,
speaking to innkeepers and publicans to
warn them not to let folk have "more drink
than would do them good," and speaking in
fairs and markets against the prevailing dishonesty and cozening.

Sharing as he did the early Puritans'
attitude towards sports and music, we find
him now, as at later periods of his life,
protesting against the revels and amusements
which seemed to him born of an evil spirit.
In this point the Quakers did not transcend
the limits of their age, and much that in its
essence we now feel to be good and helpful
to the whole life of man, was condemned by

them severely, the more readily as no doubt
the drama which they knew was the corrupt
one of the later Renaissance, and they thought
of dancing, as they so often saw it, simply as
an excuse for indulgence in luxury and for
arousing the passions of the lower nature.

But what troubled George Fox more than
the open revolt against the Divine law was
the deeper failure of the professional Christianity about him. "The earthly spirit of
the priests wounded my life," he writes, "and
when I heard the bell toll to call people
together to the steeple-house, it struck at my
life ; for it was just like a market-bell, to
gather the people together, that the priest
might set forth his ware to sale. O ! the vast
sums of money that are gotten by the trade
they make of selling the Scriptures, and by
their preaching, from the highest bishop to the
lowest priest! What one trade else in the world
is comparable to it ? Notwithstanding the
Scriptures were given forth freely and Christ
commanded His ministers to preach freely,
and the prophets and apostles denounced
judgment against all covetous hirelings and
diviners for money." [1]

With the sense of all this glowing hot
within him, there came upon him the call to

[1] Journal, i. 41.

raise his voice in protest against it. Again and again in after life he would enter a church and address the congregation, but almost always, as far as one can gather, after the preacher had ended, if preacher there was there; a practice which would seem disorderly perhaps to-day, but was general at that date, and justified by custom if not by law. On this occasion, carried away by the message that burned within him, he actually interrupted the minister before he had concluded. Fox's own words tell the story best.

"Now as I went towards Nottingham on a First day in the morning, with Friends to a Meeting there, when I came on the top of a hill in the sight of the town, I espied the great steeple-house; and the Lord said unto me, 'Thou must go cry against yonder great idol and against the worshippers therein.' I said nothing of this to the Friends that were with me, but went on with them to the Meeting, where the mighty power of the Lord was amongst us, in which I left Friends sitting in the Meeting, and I went away to the steeple-house. When I came there, all the people looked like fallow ground and the priest, like a great lump of earth, stood in his pulpit above. He took for his text these

1649

words of Peter, 'We have also a more sure
word of prophecy whereunto ye do well that
ye take heed, as unto a light that shineth in
a dark place until the day dawn, and the day
star arise in your hearts.' And he told the
people that this was the Scriptures, by which
they were to try all doctrines, religions, and
opinions. Now the Lord's power was so
mighty upon me and so strong in me, that
I could not hold, but was made to cry out
and say, ' O no, it is not the Scriptures,' and
I told them what it was, namely, the Holy
Spirit, by which the holy men of God gave
forth the Scriptures, whereby opinions,
religions, and judgments were to be tried ;
for it led into all truth, and so gave the
knowledge of all truth. The Jews had the
Scriptures and yet resisted the Holy Ghost,
and rejected Christ, the bright morning star.
They persecuted Christ and His apostles, and
took upon them to try their doctrines by the
Scriptures, but erred in judgment, and did
not try them aright, because they tried
without the Holy Ghost. As I spoke thus
amongst them the officers came and took
me away, and put me into a nasty, stinking
prison." [1]

Looking back upon the scene after all

[1] Journal, i. 42.

these years, one feels that the prophet's personality and message must be his supreme justification. Fox was one of those rare titanic natures before whom our miserable conventions shrink into nothingness.

To apologise for the breach of public order, to explain away what we may feel to have been a misinterpretation of the preacher's text, would be to misunderstand alike the man and the moment. In doing what he did George Fox was true to the highest that was in him, a message that rose immeasurably above the preacher's worthy platitudes. He was indeed acting in harmony with the advice of Paul to the Corinthian prophets, enjoining the one who might be speaking to keep silence if a revelation were given to one sitting by (1 Cor. xiv. 29, 30).

The power of Fox's message seems to have made deep impress on the congregation, and not least on the sheriff at whose house he was kept a prisoner, until he was transferred to the common jail.

Released without a trial, Fox continued his journeyings; sometimes set upon by the ignorant mob, cruelly beaten and bruised by them, with their hands, Bibles, and sticks, set in the stocks, and haled before mayors and magistrates, but now and again meeting with a friendlier response, praying with a sick man, interceding for a lunatic woman, exhorting excisemen to justice. At one time he had to meet a company of Baptists who clung to a literal interpretation of the Scriptures, at another it was a group of Pantheistic Ranters whom he strove to convince.

At length, in the autumn of 1650, he was committed by two local justices to Derby Jail, **1650** along with another Friend, for blasphemy. The immediate cause lay in his having spoken to the people at the conclusion of a public "lecture" in the church, but the justices seem to have been in doubt what to do, for Fox tells us they kept him for eight hours, sending him in and out of the court-room before they came to a decision.

"Sometimes they would tell me in a deriding manner that I was taken up in raptures. At last they asked me whether I was sanctified. I answered, 'Yes, for I was in the paradise of God.' Then they asked me if I had no sin? I answered, 'Christ my Saviour has taken away my sin, and in Him there is no sin.' They asked how we knew that Christ did abide in us? I said, 'By His Spirit that He has given us.' They temptingly asked if any of us were Christ? I answered, 'Nay, we were nothing, Christ is all.' They said, 'If a man steal, is it no sin?' I answered, 'All unrighteousness is sin.' So when they had wearied themselves in examining me they committed me and one other man to the House of Correction in Derby for six months, as blasphemers."[1]

While he was in prison, he was visited by many Puritans, who came, as he says, "to plead for sin and imperfection" with him. The jailer was at first very hostile, but one night came to confess his sorrow and beg to be allowed to lodge with his prisoner. In the night he poured out his heart to Fox and told him how he believed in the words Fox had spoken of the true faith.

Not bearing to act against his conscience longer, the jailer went next morning to the magistrates to plead for mitigation of their sentence. They granted Fox leave to walk a mile, in the hope that the troublesome prisoner would take the opportunity of escape thus afforded him, but they hardly realised the stuff of which he was made. Indeed, when his relations came in anxiety and offered bail to the extent of a hundred pounds, in those days a considerable sum, he

[1] Journal, i. 50, 51.

refused to consent to their doing this, as he would not thus make admission of guilt.

During this time Fox continued to be visited by many inquirers, amongst others by earnest-minded troopers from the army. So moved were they by the force of his character that the authorities hit upon the device of giving Fox a commission in one of the new companies which were being raised for service against Charles II. in Scotland ; his personality would attract men to join the forces, and Derby would be rid of this sturdy troubler of the existing order. It was a step which would seem scarcely strange to men in those days, when the army contained so much of the advanced wing of Puritan thought ; it was wide enough to admit Ranters and Fifth Monarchists, as well as men like Colonel John Lilburne, the Leveller, and many of the soldiers were in sympathy with some sides at least of the teaching of Fox.

But neither justices nor soldiers realised the spirit which animated the man with whom they had to deal. It is worth while to quote his own words :—

" Now the time of my commitment to the House of Correction being nearly ended, and there being many new soldiers raised, the Commissioners would have made me captain

over them ; and the soldiers said they would
have none but me. So the keeper of the
House of Correction was commanded to
bring me before the Commissioners and
soldiers in the market-place ; and there they
offered me that preferment, as they called it,
asking me if I would not take up arms for
the Commonwealth against Charles Stuart ?
I told them I knew from whence all wars
rose, even from the lust, according to James's
doctrine ; and that I lived in the virtue of
that life and power that took away the
occasion of all wars. But they courted me
to accept their offer, and thought I did but
compliment them. But I told them I was come
into the covenant of peace, which was before
wars and strifes were. They said they offered
it in love and kindness to me, because of my
virtue, and such like flattering words they
used. But I told them if that was their love
and kindness, I trampled it under my feet.
Then their rage got up, and they said,
' Take him away, jailer, and put him into the
dungeon amongst the rogues and felons.'
So I was had away and put into a lousy,
stinking place, without any bed, among
thirty felons, where I was kept almost half
a year, unless it were at times ; for they
would sometimes let me walk in the gar-

den, having a belief that I would not go away."[1]

This time of imprisonment was not, however, lost for Fox. The injustice of our legal system pressed heavily upon him as he watched the effect upon his fellow-prisoners. "I was moved to write to the judges concerning their putting men to death for cattle and money and small matters, and to show them how contrary it was to the law of God in old time; for I was under great suffering in my spirit because of it. . . . Moreover, I laid before the judges what a hurtful thing it was that prisoners should lie so long in jail; showing how they learned wickedness one of another, in talking of their bad deeds. . . ."[2]

Once again a determined effort was made by the justices to get Fox to enlist as a soldier, and he was committed once more to jail; finally, as the winter of 1651 was beginning, he was set free. From Derby he went again to his own countryside and thence to Burton and Lichfield. As he saw in the distance the spires of the Cathedral, a sense of oppression came over him: it was his duty to go to this place, he felt, and leaving his companions he set off alone. On a hill a mile from the town

1651

[1] Journal, i. 68.   [2] i. 70, 71.

he left his boots with some shepherds, though it was winter time, and walked barefoot into Lichfield.

It was market-day, but no one laid hands on him as he passed up and down the streets crying, "Woe to the bloody city of Lichfield!" and as he went it seemed to him as though a channel of blood ran through the streets, and stood red in the market-place. And so he passed back again to the shepherds, without understanding the meaning of his message.

It is the one incident in the life of Fox which seems to tell of a brain overwrought, overtaxed with the hardships through which he had passed, or with that mental and spiritual struggle through which he had entered into peace. It seems, too, to have been a thing over which he himself puzzled, for he notes the deep consideration which came upon him as to the cause of what he had been sent to do. "For though Parliament had the minster, one while, and the King another, and much blood had been shed in the town during the wars between them, yet that was no more than had befallen many other places. But afterwards I came to understand that in the Emperor Diocletian's time, a thousand Christians were martyred in Lichfield. So I was to go without my shoes, through the channel of their blood, and unto the pool of their blood in the market-place, that I might raise up the memorial of the blood of those martyrs which had been shed above a thousand years before, and lay cold in their streets. . . ." [1]

The struggle at Lichfield between the two parties in the war had been peculiarly fierce and bitter, and doubtless the embers of hatred and ill-will were still warm ; something of this the stranger may have felt as he uttered his words of denunciation. The explanation which in later years he himself thought the right one, is one which has been dismissed as fanciful by more recent writers. Yet, however much exaggeration there may have been in the story of the persecution under Diocletian, the name of the city, " The Field of Corpses," points to some tragedy in the far-off past whose echoes may in some way we hardly understand have reached his inward ear ; his mind was dimly conscious of some terrible scene of cruelty and bloodshed, and his heart rose in protest against it, as against that spirit of persecution which was still alive in the hearts of many of the citizens of Lichfield.

[1] Journal, i. 78, 79.

The next few years were full of fruitful
service for Fox. He passed up and down
holding meetings, and was thus the means of
convincing a number of men afterwards well
known in the new Society; especially was
this the case in the North of England, where
in Yorkshire Richard Farnsworth, James
Nayler, and William Dewsbury joined the
ranks of the Quakers. In the East Riding
he was more than once the guest of a friendly
magistrate, Justice Hotham, and he visited
many of the churches of the district to speak
to the people after the minister had ended
his sermon. Sometimes, as at York, the outcome was that he was attacked by an angry
mob, but the result was often far different,
so that a lady of Justice Hotham's ac-
quaintance told him how "there came an
angel or spirit unto the church at Beverley
and spoke the wonderful things of God, to
the astonishment of all that were there; and
when it had done, it passed away, and they
did not know whence it came, nor whither it
went, but it astonished all, both priests, professors, and magistrates of the town."[1]
Sometimes the minister of the church himself
was so moved as to confess the truth of the
stranger's message, or even to go further, like

[1] Journal, i. 81.

Philip Scafe, of Staithes, whom "the Lord by His free Spirit did afterwards make a free minister of His free Gospel." [1]   At Pickering an old clergyman hailed him as brother, accompanying him from place to place to his own church on the moors, and thence onward.

But it was not always such easy work, and Fox had often to sleep out in the fields, and sometimes had difficulty in getting the people to sell him food. On more than one occasion friendly magistrates offered to interfere to punish the men who had wronged him, but Fox always refused to appear against them, even when he had been beaten and dragged through the street and stoned and struck till he was covered with blood.

It was amongst the yeomen of the northern dales apparently that Fox found his most numerous converts. Passing beyond Settle, though he had eaten little for some days, he climbed Pendle Hill, and looking down upon the country before him, the Lord, he tells us, let him see in what places He had a great people to be gathered. [2]

In the neighbourhood of Sedbergh there was soon a large congregation of Friends gathered together, and hard by, at Firbank

[1] Journal, i. 86.   [2] i. 109

Chapel in Westmorland, two local independent ministers, John Audland
1652 and Francis Howgill, became converts to the Quaker teaching. They had
both been preaching in the chapel in the
morning, and in the afternoon they and their
congregation gathered round George Fox, as
he sat on a rock hard by, and the numbers
grew until it was thought there were above a
thousand there. For well nigh three hours
they listened as Fox spoke to them of the
Spirit of God in themselves, of the ideals of
early Christianity and the apostasy that later
had entered into the Church. They were not
to wonder at his preaching on the hillside
instead of in their chapel, for there was no
peculiar holiness in any building ; God's
true temples were not houses of stone, but
hearts of men, and His priesthood free and
open to all, not confined to one class or
supported by enforced tithes. " The Lord's
convincing power," adds Fox, " accompanied
my ministry, and reached the hearts of the
people, whereby many were convinced, and
all the teachers of that congregation, who
were many, were convinced of God's everlasting truth." [1]

Passing into Furness through Westmorland,

[1] Journal, i. 115.

where at Underbarrow he had some discussion with the Presbyterian preacher,
Edward Burrough, shortly to become one of
the most eminent of the Quaker ministers,
George Fox came now to Ulverstone and the
adjoining hamlet of Swarthmore.

At Swarthmore Hall lived one of the
most influential commoners in the North
of England—Judge Thomas Fell, a close
friend of Bradshaw; since 1645 he had
been a member of the Long Parliament, and
was now one of Cromwell's judges of the
Welsh Circuit, and shortly to become
Chancellor of the Duchy of Lancaster.
He was married to a Lancashire lady,
Margaret Askew, a woman of exceptional
power of character. The Judge was from
home on circuit, and his wife was absent
for the day, but they were accustomed,
as she tells us, to entertain any travelling preachers and "religious people" who
visited that part of the country, and George
Fox was brought by a friend of his to
the hospitable house. He had some discussion with the clergyman of Ulverstone,
William Lampitt, and when Mrs. Fell returned at night she was troubled to learn of
the dispute, as she had been an earnest
follower of Mr. Lampitt. They had further

talk together on the subject, and then on a
fast day in the church at Ulverstone the
opportunity came to see things in a new
light.

The congregation had been gathered for
some time before Fox entered. " When I
came," he writes, " Lampitt was singing with
his people, but his spirit was so foul, and the
matter they sang so unsuitable to their states,
that after they had done singing, I was moved
of the Lord to speak to him and the people." [1]
Margaret Fell has given us a vivid picture of
the scene. " When they were singing before
the sermon he came in, and when they had
done singing he stood up upon a seat or
form, and desired that he might have liberty
to speak, and he that was in the pulpit said
he might. And the first words that he spoke
were as followeth : ' He is not a Jew that is
one outward ; neither is that circumcision
which is outward, but he is a Jew that is one
inward, and that is circumcision which is of
the heart.' And so he went on, and said how
that Christ was the Light of the world, and
lighteth every man that cometh into the
world, and that by this light they might be
gathered to God, &c. I stood up in my pew
and wondered at his doctrine, for I had never

[1] Journal, i. 119.

heard such before. And then he went on and
opened the Scriptures, and said : ' The Scriptures were the prophets' words, and Christ's
and the apostles' words, and what as they
spoke they enjoyed, and possessed . . . then
what had any to do with the Scriptures, but
as they came to the Spirit that gave them
forth? You will say, Christ saith this, and
the apostles say this, but what canst thou
say? . . . What thou speakest is it inwardly
from God?'

" This opened me so that it cut me to the
heart, and then I saw clearly we were all
wrong. So I sat down in my pew again, and
cried bitterly, and I cried in my spirit to the
Lord, 'We are all thieves, we are all thieves ;
we have taken the Scriptures in words, and
know nothing of them in ourselves.' "

She was but dimly conscious, she tells us,
of his going on to denounce the false prophets
and priests of the present day, and of the
Puritan justice, John Sawrey, calling upon
the churchwardens to take him away. Fox
tells us how she protested on his behalf,
Lampitt himself also calling out, " Let him
speak." Finally Sawrey lost patience, and
ordered the constable to remove the troublesome preacher, and Fox concluded his words
to the people in the graveyard without.

Fox went on upon his missionary tour, and shortly afterwards two other Quaker preachers —Richard Farnsworth and James Nayler— came to Swarthmore, and aided the new converts greatly.

The Judge was met upon his home-coming with the unwelcome news that his wife and family were bewitched by these meddlesome strangers. Judge Fell returned to his house highly displeased and not a little prejudiced against the Quaker fanatics, but after some talk with them he was better satisfied. At night George Fox arrived, and with the Judge's assent a meeting was held in the parlour of the Hall, at which Fox spoke. Next day there was a little gathering of Quakers at the house, and as they were discussing where they could hold their meetings Judge Fell broke in with the invitation, "You may meet here if you will." For some time his attitude was rather one of kindly toleration to his wife's friends than of approval, and he rode alone with his serving-man to church to attend the parish services, but after a while his point of view changed, and, discontinuing all other attendance at places of worship, he would sit in his little inner room with the door open, while the Friends met in the great parlour adjoining, listening to the words spoken, and doubtless sharing in their quiet waiting upon God. So until his death in 1658 Judge Fell was able to be of great use to the growing company of Quakers in Westmorland and Lancashire in mitigating to some extent the persecution to which they were subjected, and in influencing the magistrates towards greater leniency.

Swarthmore Hall thus became a centre to which Quaker preachers might return, after long months of travel and hard usage, broken by frequent imprisonments. There they were always sure of a welcome and of safety from persecution, from which the Judge's position shielded them with even greater security than might have been the case had he actually joined their number.

But though the existence of such a spot—almost the only place in England where a Quaker might rest secure—was doubtless of great importance in the growth of the new movement, the thought of fleeing from persecution was far from the minds of these pioneers of liberty and conscience. What was of much greater importance to Fox and his fellow-preachers was the knowledge that here they had a settled congregation of worshippers in full sympathy with them, with numerous similar groups in the surrounding

5

countryside, forming a centre where they might always find the help of fellowship and the spiritual refreshment which they needed when weary of heart. Often, too, the consciousness of the life there must have helped them when cut off from the world in prison and far from outward fellowship. We may think of the little circle which met regularly in worship at Swarthmore henceforth as the altar fire from which the light of the Quaker message was borne by many a brave preacher up and down the land; hither they could always return to kindle afresh another torch.

Apart from this deepest of all helps, Swarthmore Hall was a centre of information for the first generation of Quakers. The travelling preachers corresponded much with one another, but more than with any other with Margaret Fell. Often indeed to write to her was the surest way to communicate with each other, for at any moment one and another might be cast into jail as they journeyed from place to place.

Fox did not stay long now at Swarthmore, but went on this side and that through Furness and Westmorland, preaching with the most far-reaching results. Convert after convert, not a few of them from amongst the ministers who opposed him, presently obeyed a call to proclaim the same message.

III

THE MESSAGE OF EARLY QUAKERISM

A SKETCH of the early Quaker movement, however slight, would be incomplete without some expression of the message which its preachers proclaimed.

In attempting to realise what the teaching of the early Quakers meant one is met at the outset by what seems an almost unsurmountable obstacle in the bewildering mass of books and pamphlets whose very titles prove a terror to the bibliographer (for not a few extend to two closely-printed pages), and whose contents provide in many cases still greater difficulties to the modern reader, in their formless disregard of style and grammar, if not in the reiteration and incoherence of their thoughts. Yet the very absence of real literature amongst the larger part of the writings of the early Friends may help us to see more

clearly their true message, which was one
lived rather than written, passed on from soul
to soul by directer and deeper channels than
the narrow roads of logic. The more we see
the roughness of the tools used, the more
clearly we shall perceive the Divine power
that was with them, and made them what
they were.

One thing that cannot fail to strike the
most superficial student of the early Quaker
writers is their intense conviction. They
speak with authority as having firm hold of
Him who is invisible. They are prophets,
denouncing the evil and opening up the way
of truth as messengers of God. And with a
spirit like that of the old martyrs of the early
days of the Church, they rejoiced in their
sufferings, and went cheerfully through the
fire of persecution and the storm of calumny
and hate. What was it all for? we ask.

Throughout the writings of the early
Friends runs one all-pervading, overpowering
thought—that of the Light within. In every
human heart, they tell us, there speaks the
voice of God, and we have heard Him. The
Light of Christ shines still for all men in the
inmost of their souls, and in obedience to its
influence lies hope for every man, whether
Pagan, Christian, or Jew. Somewhere at the

back of all our lives, in us but not of us, there shines a ray of that Divine Life which was given to the world in all fulness in Jesus of Nazareth. If we obey this Light of Christ in our hearts, even though our knowledge be most incomplete, the Divine Life that witnesses to the evil within and inspires to good will flow through us, guiding us to truth, and bring to birth a new nature within us, which conquers sin and overcomes evil with good.

This is the unseen work of the Spirit of Christ in the heart, and in this Divine Light alone does all the revelation hitherto given to men become real to us, which without it were no true revelation at all. It is only by sharing in a measure the Spirit through which all inspired Scripture was written that we come to understand what the Scriptures mean. Without this we might know about, but only thus can we know.

The Gospel of early Quakerism was a religion universal and real ; something which all men needed and which the poorest and most ignorant could understand, which could make the weakest strong. It was the realisation of the words of the Master, " The Kingdom of God is within you," " the Kingdom of God is with power." It appealed to the hearts of all

because all had within them the Divine witness. " To that of God in your consciences I
speak," George Fox would say, again and
again, as he strove to convince his adversaries.

What the early Friends preached was, they
tell us, " Primitive Christianity revived " ; the
professional Christianity of their day appeared
to them unreal ; they were sensible that there
had been a great apostasy from the ideals
and methods of the early Church, and that
because there was apostasy from the Spirit
of Christ. Something of this feeling may, I
believe, be traced from the very earliest days
in the history of the successive movements in
the life of the Church, which are now branded
as heresies or honoured as reformations.
The Montanists in the days of Tertullian, the
Paulicians in later times, and in the Middle
Ages, St. Francis within the Church and the
Catharists and Waldensians without it, alike
appealed from the corruption and laxness of
official Christianity to the purity and simpli-
city of Christ. There is no need to show
how Wyclif and Luther did the same. And
of these, the ones to whom the early Friends
seem most near in spirit did much more than
make an appeal to a higher moral standard
or to a truer view of doctrine. They were

strong because they came into direct touch themselves with the Unseen. They did not take their faith from others, but were led by the Spirit of God themselves. The contrast is no new one between the orthodox moral Christianity of the organised Church and the living Christianity of the men who are rebuked or despised as misguided fanatics, and perhaps abused as heretics by their own generation, and afterwards honoured as heroes and saints, though the spirit of their message may be disregarded.

The story of early Quakerism is that of one long battle. Through deep travail of soul George Fox had come, before the great Light shone clearly in his heart ; and then he had his religion at first hand. All about him he found seekers discontented with second-hand truths ; their fingers were already groping at the shutters of the soul's windows, and they had but to open them for God's daylight to come in. The natural result for them all was that when once they had thus felt the power of God's touch in their own lives, and the reality of communion with Him in their hearts, they ceased to ask help from the teacher who could only tell them about God at third hand, whose sole knowledge came from the instruction of others, whether by word of mouth or through the written page, even though that written page might be the Bible. And they could not stop there ; they had to help to persuade the unwilling mind, too, to open its windows, and they knew that somehow or other it could always be done, just because no soul was altogether ceiled up from the Light ; somewhere through some chink or cranny one Divine ray at least was pouring in, and all they had to do was to find that place, and get the hindrances moved away within and without, so that more light might come in. When they looked at the orthodox traditional Christianity about them, they found that what hindered people from seeing the light was often not so much the living errors as the old dead truths. Such people were content with religion at fourth hand, doled out to them by teachers who only got it at third hand themselves. The Quaker could never be content with a regular supply of certified truth dealt out like medicine from a physician's hand.

He had found the fountain of all truth and felt the power and life of Christ in his own heart ; how then could he have unity with teachers who admitted that their whole knowledge of God came from the Scriptures and the writings of pious men? And what wonder that the controversy between the early Friends and their orthodox opponents was so acute on both sides?

As we turn over the pages of those old pamphlets in which they waged war on one another, we cannot but regret their harshness, and sometimes the confidence with which the Quakers proclaimed their prophetic character may shock us, who are so cautious and lukewarm in expressing our own convictions. But I believe the impartial critic (and it is not easy for any member of the Society to be impartial in this) will not hesitate to say on which side there is more of Christian charity.

"*Hell broken loose; or a history of the Quakers,*" are the opening words of the title of a pamphlet by Thomas Underhill, citizen and stationer of London; "*Quakerism no Christianity,*" "*The Pilgrim's Progress from Quakerism to Christianity,*" "*The thorough Quaker no Christian,*" stand out among the titles of books written against the early Quakers, who, though their replies were often strong enough in their language, were yet able to write "Friend," or at least "Poor Souls," in addressing their opponents.

But if it does nothing else, this very bitterness helps us to realise the depth of the gulf

which separates the two parties ; a bitterness
which one finds repeated in the history of
similar movements, like Methodism in the
eighteenth century or Quietism on the
Continent at the close of the seventeenth, in
both of which one of the great points, if not
the centre of dispute, lay in the claim made
by the innovators to a direct personal communion with the Divine, and an individual
experience which their opponents considered
to be presumptuous and founded on fanatical
delusion if not on wilful deceit.[1]

These instances alone will show that the
great central fact of the Quaker movement
was not altogether peculiar to it ; but this
was indeed a claim made by the early Friends
themselves. What they preached was the
Christianity of the first golden years which
had been realised again in part at least by
the martyrs of truth down all the ages. They
claimed kinship willingly with Lollard heretic
and persecuted Catholic Quietist, and would
surely have rejoiced in much too of the
message to which the old Methodists a
hundred years later bore witness, or in that
of Stundists and Dukhobors in the present

[1] Cf. pastoral letter of Robert Lowth, Bishop of
London, on Whitefield's Journal (" A Caution
against Enthusiasm ").

day. It may be doubted, perhaps, whether they would have felt equally at home amid the comfortable societies of our own time, or whether we should not have felt a little afraid of the daring spirit, the uncompromising out-spokenness, the intensity, and the fire of the Quakers of the first generation.

There can be, I think, no doubt that the central doctrine of Quakerism, is that of the Universal and saving Light of Christ. The supreme place given by the early Friends to the Light of Christ in the heart, was felt in their own lives before it was understood as a philosophical principle, and from it depends all that distinguished the practical ethics of Quakerism.

The philosophical attitude, the theology and life theory of Quakerism, is bound up with a fact of individual experience. It is no " theory in the air," assented to by an act of the intellectual faculties, which may be dis-pelled by exercise of logic or upset by over-whelming argument. It is rather an attitude of soul resulting from inward experience, and necessarily affecting the whole conduct of life in every way.

All the peculiarities of the early Quakers, in so far as they were not merely those of the Puritan age, conditioned by the limitations

of the day, may be traced to this one central
principle : the immediate revelation of Christ
in every heart, and the consequent call for
the submission of the whole life to the Divine
source of Light and power, and to no other
guide.

After all, with the deepest aspect of the
great truth of the central doctrine of Quakerism words cannot deal. Language fails to
express that which goes beyond all the effort
of our intellect to follow. Spirit speaks to
Spirit, and only he who is born of the Spirit
can understand something of what that birth
means. Thus the early Friends seemed constantly to make an appeal in their missionary
work to the Divine spark of Light in the
souls of their hearers, that like might respond
to like. "To that of God in you I speak,"
writes George Fox ; "I directed men to the
Light of Christ in their hearts." The preacher
was only an instrument to put the hearer in
touch with God ; he was not to draw men to
himself, but to turn them to the deeper
source of all power ; his part was to seek
out amidst his hearers the conductive strands
which were capable of receiving the heavenly
electricity, and when once the listeners were
in touch with that, his own work was done.
"To take men to Christ and leave them

there" was George Fox's explanation of the aim of ministry.

Let us consider briefly something of what this meant in its application to religious thought and to the conduct of life. We naturally ask ourselves in what it was that the Christianity of George Fox differed from that of Baxter and Bunyan, good men and zealous opponents as they were.

George Fox records as the first great revelation that came to him, the learning of the truth, that true belief meant the passing from death to life. "About the beginning of the year 1646, as I was going to Coventry, and approaching towards the gate, a consideration arose in me how it was said that 'all Christians are believers, both Protestants and Papists,' and the Lord opened to me that if all were believers, then they were all born of God, and passed from death to life, and that none were true believers but such; and though others said they were believers, yet they were not."[1] The Puritans about him might not have expressed themselves as he did, but they, many of them, surely knew themselves too this new birth of the soul, and the Friends were willing to recognise this, although sometimes they did not perceive

[1] Journal, i. 7.

it in individuals whose names we honour now. But though the Puritans often went through the same spiritual experience, they bound their new life fast in swaddling clothes, and their whole religious system was so wrapped about it as to hinder and prevent its growth. They had felt the Divine touch in their lives, but instead of surrendering themselves freely to it, they looked for human guidance instead. They sought help from their learned preachers and theologians, and they searched the Scriptures thinking to find eternal life in them, instead of in the living Christ of whom they testified.

They were at best content often to be fed upon the milk with which their spiritual life began, and were too timid to seek the solid food for which it was meant to prepare them. They did not dare to open their minds to a new truth, and because they did not think of the old truth as living truth, it too often became dead to them,—and is not a dead truth often the most dangerous form of falsehood?

Practically, too, there was one great difference between Quaker and Puritan, in the optimism of the one as compared with the pessimistic convictions of the other. The Quaker knew that at any moment he might fall into sin, if he did not abide faithfully in the light and power of his Lord, but he believed that his Master was a real God, whose power could go to the roots of his life and keep him from the evil ; if he fell, it was his fault, not God's.   Sin could be constantly overcome by the indwelling power of Christ and the command of the Saviour, " Be ye therefore perfect, even as your Father in Heaven is perfect," was not given in bitter irony, but with a real purpose.   For if indwelling sin was to be ever blackening the life of the true Christian, in the way the Puritans pictured it, the moral law became a cruel mockery, and all effort after holiness hollow and vain.

It was contended by the opponents of the Quakers that their doctrine of the light of Christ within tended to make them neglect the revelation of God to man in the past recorded in the Scriptures, and to disregard the historic manifestation of Christ and the work of His life and death.

Yet neglect of the study of the Scriptures was certainly no fault of the early Quakers. Often enough they were able to make it clear that they knew their Bibles better than their adversaries.   And indeed the position they took up was the only one by which the Scrip-

tures could be truly honoured. Their orthodox opponents were in danger of making
an idol of a Book, but failed to see that it
was only as the Spirit of Truth made its
messages living and real to their minds that
the Bible could bring to them words from God.

And so too in regard to belief in the historic Christ, the Quakers felt that the professing orthodox Christians about them were
honouring a far-off Saviour who was not
realised as having any actual and present
influence on their lives, whether they thought
of Him as having lived and died in a distant
land in an age long passed away, or as existing in infinite glory in a heaven that was
altogether remote from their daily work, in
another world that they would only know
after death or at the Last Day.

It was as though, in its exaltation of the
Scriptures as " the word of God," and in its
unliving worship of the historic Christ, the
professing Church had built a hundred beautiful shrines over the places where God had
once spoken to men, and a great cathedral
over the spot where the dead Christ had lain,
only to make it clearer that God no longer
spoke to His people now, and that Jesus of
Nazareth was passed far away from the lives
of men.

But the early Quakers could not thus shut God out of His world, nor be content to worship a dead Saviour. The Almighty speaks still, they tell us, to the listening ear, and Christ is alive, and not dead. By making the Scriptures the only revelation of God, the Puritans brought it about too often that they ceased to be a revelation at all, because when revelation is not present and actual its very meaning vanishes away; while because the Quakers knew that God speaks to all men and had never ceased to instruct His Church, the Scriptures became to them true channels of revelation, and their messages quivered with life. The Bible took its right place, not as a wonderful God-made book, fallen from heaven among men, without a parallel of any kind, and with nothing in our lives to correspond to its revelation, but as the unique revelation amidst a never-ending series of revelations, containing the history of God's dealings with men exemplified in the story of the nation which had listened best to His voice and had in some measure risen to its call to be the medium of revelation to others; above all, as containing the great record of God's supreme self-manifestation to man in Christ, and of His work for us, to which the Light in all our hearts calls us to respond.

6

The life of Christ on earth was to the Puritan an event utterly isolated; "die Eingreifung Gottes in die Geschichte," to use the modern phrase of Herrmann.

But to the Quaker, God's hand was not thrust once only into this universe of His, but is always working there ; He reveals Himself to every man through the Light of Christ in the heart, and it is just because of this inner Light that the supreme manifestation of God in the Incarnation can make appeal to us. If Christ's own nature were not at work in our hearts through this Divine Light, it would remain foreign to us and utterly apart ; the Incarnation would be useless, because we could never understand it. It is only as the Light works in our heart that we get any true idea of the Incarnation at all. For the darkness cannot comprehend the Light, and it is because the Light goes on shining still that we are able to see. We could never know that God was in Christ reconciling the world to Himself if it were not for the answering witness of the Spirit of God in our souls.

With this all-embracing Gospel in their hearts it was small wonder that the early Friends were eager to carry their message to the whole world, making essay, for instance, to win over the Pope to the truth, whether by writing him epistles or by making pilgrimage to Rome; and George Fox's letters to the Dey of Algiers, the Grand Cham, and the Emperor of China represent the same spirit, which was not wholly without its reward. Mary Fisher, when she visited the Sultan, was received with honour as a prophetess; and we know from the journal of John Woolman, how, in later days, a true Quaker preacher found his way direct to the heart of the unlettered Indian. One wonders what the result might have been had such Quaker missionaries been able to find an audience amongst those Eastern nations whose mode of thought seems one to which the true spiritual Christianity should appeal in a peculiar way, though they are repelled by the intellectual system of orthodox dogmatics and by the ecclesiastical organisation of the great Western Churches.

But no view of the central doctrine of Quakerism would be adequate which did not allude to the effect it had upon the worship and the whole life of the men who held it.

The reality of personal communion between the soul and God through Christ's unseen presence in the heart rendered it needless to insist on the observance of external forms and conditions, which at best

could only be channels of the grace of God;
and he who had heard the Divine voice call
him, and been given his message by the Master
did not need to have it granted him by any
other authority. Nor could the brotherhood
of the Church exclude any men or women
from any work to which they had received
the heavenly call, under pretext of inca-
pacity arising from sex or station. All true
Christians must be in touch with God, and
the organisation of the Church should be
such as to help them to obey Him and fulfil
whatever service He calls them to, as simply
as might be. Ministry then could never be
confined to one fixed class, still less treated
as the subject for bargains and money-
making.

And the gatherings of the Church for
worship must be free too, as times when the
children of the kingdom are gathered together
to meet with the Father and to hear His
voice, and if He call them to it, to hand on
His message to others. It was not possible
then that these meetings should be fettered
by fixed liturgies however beautiful, for they
must needs be often chains, though chains of
jewelled gold.

And since this communion of the soul with
the Divine was to be no mere isolated event,

but its normal attitude, the whole life had to be altered and raised to the level of the times specially set apart for worship. All days were the Lord's days, and all life His. He gives His Light freely to all men, and the children of the Light must not yield to the false conventions and the pagan organisations of society which tend against the realisation of human brotherhood. So dishonesty and ill-will to our fellow-men must be banished from our lives as we submit ourselves to the Light of Christ, the spirit of war replaced by the spirit of peace, and the spirit of falsehood by the Spirit of Truth which will not suffer us to have a twofold standard, one for Sundays, and for what we swear to as in God's presence, and the other for week-days and our ordinary intercourse with men, from which all thought of God is far removed. The relationship of Christian to Christian within the Church is not to be harshly opposed to the Christian's relations with those outside, for the life of the Church is but the earnest and foretaste of the life that shall some day reign throughout all the world.

Christ's light shines in every soul and the whole life must be submitted freely to His guidance. As the love of God goes out to

every man, all the world over, as He cares
for all, however poor and bad and wretched,
so those who are called by the name of
Christ must let the same all-embracing love
enter their whole lives.   Friends to the truth
must be friends to all men.   Such was the
programme of Christianity as conceived by
the early Quakers.

IV

THE GROWTH OF THE NEW MOVEMENT

THE years 1653 to 1656 were above all others those of the great outburst of Quaker missionary activity which carried the movement all over England and across the seas to America. From this point the history of Quakerism must be concerned with many other lives than that of Fox, although he still remains the dominating figure around whose story we can more fittingly group some glimpses of his co-workers.

From the dales and fells and from the countrysides of the North went out a band of preachers whose names are hardly known to the historian, but whose lives and teaching had the deepest influence on seventeenth-century England. Simple yeomen most of them, whose message came more strongly through the spoken word than the written

page; men whose writings make difficult
reading after two centuries and a half of
time, but of whose spirit we can in some
measure get glimpses in the brief spiritual
autobiographies which not a few left behind
them, and in the "testimonies" which their
friends published after their death to bear
witness to the truth for which they had
lived.

At the commencement of the eighteenth
century a systematic attempt was made to
collect from the survivors of the early days
some record of the men who first brought the
Quaker message to the different parts of the
country, and the Friends' Historical Society
is now publishing the manuscript collection
of replies which the different Quarterly Meetings throughout England sent in response to
the request of the Yearly Meeting. This
collection of *The First Publishers of Truth*,
as it was called, gives most interesting
evidence of the way in which comparatively
unknown men were the means by which the
new gospel spread from town to town. In
some cases they would speak at the market-
cross, or in the parish church, but frequently
they seem to have gone to some meeting
of Independents or Baptists where there was
greater freedom of prophesying, and where

the minds of the hearers were more open to receive fresh views of truth. The collection is all too succinct, but here and there the writers give a glimpse of how the message came.

Thus at Leominster we read:[1] "In or about the year 1655 came a servant of the Lord, but a stranger outwardly, called Thomas Parrish, but of what parts no account can be given now, into a meeting of the people called Independents, who were met on the first day of the week at the house of Colonel James, at Tripleton. And after some time he had waited on the Lord in spirit, he had an opportunity to speak, all being silent; he said by way of exhortation, 'Keep to the Lord's watch.' These words, being spake in the power of God, had its operation upon all or most of the meeting, so that they felt some great dread and fear upon their spirits, and being silent for some space of time, some thought to have spake as usually to the meeting but could not because of the unusual awe that was on their spirits; so after a little time he spake again saying, 'What I say unto you, I say unto all, watch.' Then [he] was silent again a little time, but the whole meeting, being

[1] *The First Publishers of Truth*, pp. 115, 116.

sensible that this man was in some extraordinary spirit and power, were all musing
what manner of teaching this should be,
being such a voice that most of the hearers
never heard before, that carried such great
authority with it that they were all necessi-
tated to be subject to the power, though it
was a great cross to their wills to sit in
silence, though it was but a little time.
Then he spake again these words, or to this
purpose, 'Where are your minds now?
wandering abroad? Or in the spirit,
watching with the Lord?' Then he went
on and opened the great mystery of God's
salvation, turning their minds to the spirit
of Christ, by which some of them knew he
spake the truth, in the inward parts, which
was the Light that shined in their hearts.
Then one in the meeting, whose heart God
had opened, bare this testimony to the truth,
saying that he blessed God that he had
heard the voice of His Spirit that day, though
he knew not the man outwardly, nor what
religion he professed. . . ."

Readier still was the welcome given to the
new preachers by such companies of seekers
as Charles Marshall describes in his Journal,
when he was a lad of seventeen in Bristol:
" And in those times which was about the

year 1654 there were many which were
seeking after the Lord; and there were a
few of us that kept one day of the week
in fasting and prayer, so that when this day
came we met together early in the morning
not tasting anything, and sat down sometimes in silence; and as any found a concern on their spirits and inclination in their
hearts they knelt down and sought the Lord;
so that sometimes before the day ended there
might be twenty of us might pray; men and
women, and sometimes children spake a few
words in prayer: and we were sometimes
greatly bowed and broken before the Lord,
in humility and tenderness. And unto one
of these meetings, in the year 1654, came
dearly beloved John Audland and John
Camm, Messengers of the Everlasting
God. . . ." [1]

These two ministers were those convinced
in 1652 through the ministry of George Fox,
at Firbank Chapel in Westmorland; they
were neighbours and close friends in their
new labours, travelling up together to interview the Protector on behalf of the persecuted
Quakers, and later journeying to Bristol, which
became the centre of their field of ministry.
John Audland, though younger by twenty

[1] Marshall, *Sion's Travellers Comforted*, 1704, 8vo.

years than his friend, had already achieved
reputation as an eloquent preacher in his
county at the time of his convincement, and
had then to go through an experience very
like that which befell the great mystic,
Tauler, three hundred years before. For a
time he felt only his own helplessness, but
after some weeks of deep sadness the power
which had touched his life found utterance,
and thenceforth he devoted himself to the
work of the ministry ungrudgingly; the two
friends did indeed give their lives to the
work, and in 1656, John Camm, who was
naturally weak in body, died, spent with the
toil of travel and open-air preaching, but
with a heart at rest and full of joy. John
Audland continued his labours, undergoing
repeated imprisonments and ill-usage, and
dying in 1664, when little more than thirty-
four years old. [1]

[1] It is of interest to note that it was in connection
with the introduction of Quakerism in Bristol that
the curious belief arose that the Quakers were Roman
Catholic emissaries in disguise ; a misrepresentation
which for two generations did not wholly disappear.
An affidavit was even made that Franciscan friars
from Rome had been recognised preaching in the
Friends' Meetings. An amusing attack upon them
based upon this will be found in William Prynne's
" The Quakers unmasked and clearly detected to be

In 1652 and the years that followed we
must picture a like work as proceeding in
almost every part of the country. In the
Eastern Counties the Westmorland yeoman,
Richard Hubberthorne, was followed by his
fellow-countryman, George Whitehead, and
both were imprisoned in Norwich Jail. In
this case very different lives of service
awaited the two preachers. Hubberthorne
was cast into Newgate in 1662 by Alderman
Sir Richard Brown, and was one of the
many victims who died in that overcrowded
and pestilent spot ; yet in such peace of soul
that it is recorded "that it was not remem-
bered that he groaned all the time of his
sickness." [1] A striking picture of the man—
"Dear, innocent Richard," as George Fox
called him—is given by his fellow-prisoner,
Edward Burrough. "He was but little in
stature in his outward man, and of weak
constitution of body, and was slow of speech
and often more ready to hear than to speak ;
he made little appearances in the manhood
of excellency or authority, but was con-
temptible among men, yet he was very wise

but the spawn of Romish frogs, Jesuites and Franciscan Freers ; sent from Rome to seduce the intoxicated,
giddy-pated English nation," 1654, 4to.

[1] *Piety Promoted*, vol. 1. p. 50, ed. 1723.

and knew his season when to speak and when
to be silent . . . and his ministry was often
savoury and seasonable and felt in the pure
life, though his words were plain and homely." [1]

It was the lot of George Whitehead to
live through all the persecutions of the
Commonwealth and Restoration, sharing in
the troubles that overtook the Friends so
fully that for a long time during the reign of
Charles II. he was accustomed never to go
to meeting without a nightcap in his pocket,
as never knowing whether the conventicle
might not be broken up and himself lodged
in jail. After the death of Fox he became
almost the most prominent of the Quaker
leaders, and lived to present an address to
George I. in the name of the Society long
after most of the Friends of his early days
had passed away, dying peacefully, after a
full life of service, in 1723.

While these Friends were active in the
East of England, Thomas Holmes journeyed
into Wales, Miles Halhead into Scotland,
and afterwards, in company with Thomas
Salthouse, into Devon and Cornwall, while a
number of preachers travelled through the
various parts of Yorkshire.

[1] A collection of the several books . . . of R.
Hubberthorne, 1663, 4to,

Some idea of the intense earnestness of their mission may be gathered from the words of a convert who afterwards shared in their labours. Thomas Thomson tells us how at Christmastide in 1652, Thomas Stubbs and William Dewsbury parted from each other to go to the different parts to which they felt drawn. " We sat down and were in prayer and supplication to the Lord much of the day, William labouring to strengthen Thomas and encourage him in the exercise and service for the Lord till about the third hour in the afternoon ; so the day being far spent Thomas took leave and departed towards Beverley. Then William and I made ready for our journey towards Malton ; but William's care and travel being great for the prosperity of Sion, we got not to our Friends there till after the setting of the sun ; then having twelve or thirteen miles to go, we set forwards, and many times run upon the wolds ; and it being a clear, moonshine night we got to Malton about the eighth or ninth hour of the night. There we found brethren and Friends assembled in the house of Robert Hebden, Richard Farnsworth (another travelling Friend in the ministry) being there with them ; so we were greatly comforted and refreshed in the love of God with our friends that night." [1]

These men lived indeed in the spirit of prayer, and one cannot altogether wonder at such a scene as the same writer goes on to describe when in 1656 John Whitehead held for the first time a Friends' meeting at Hunvanby (now Hunmanby) on the Wolds. The roughs of the village threw stones at the people who came together in the little close where the meeting was to be held, so that they withdrew into a barn for quiet. There John Whitehead spoke with power, but presently the angry crowd without burst into the room raging and cursing. The Friends present stood close around the preacher, who continued unmoved. One after another those who stood between him and the mob were dragged and thrust away until, as they were close to him, the intruders suddenly stopped still, turned their backs and left the room. Quiet fell upon the little gathering, and after a time of silent prayer the preacher spoke again, and the first Quaker meeting in Hunmanby closed in a sense of the power of the Divine presence over all.

It is difficult to describe the early years of

[1] T. Thomson's testimony in *The Written Gospel Labours of John Whitehead*, London, 1704, 8vo.

the Society of Friends apart from the story
of individual lives, but one realises how independent the Quaker movement was of the
machinery of organised leadership, and how
deep in the life of the people was the need
which it met, as one reads such a story as
that of the convincement of the sailor,
Thomas Lurting. He was boatswain's mate
on one of Blake's men-of-war, and tells us
in his autobiography how a soldier who had
been at a meeting in Scotland first brought
news of the Quakers' teaching to his ship ;
though this man stayed but a short time with
them, after some six months' time one or two
of the crew began to meet in silence together
for worship instead of coming to hear the
chaplain, and gradually, in spite of punishments from the captain and persecution from
their fellow sailors, one after another joined
the little band. Equally remarkable was
the way in which, quite without having any
knowledge of a like trend of thought amongst
the Quakers in England, these men, whom
the captain had at length come to regard as
the most daring and trustworthy fighters on
his ship, came almost all at once to realise
that they could no longer endeavour to take
the lives of their fellow-men. The story of
their heroism in remaining faithful to their

convictions, and of the later adventures of
Lurting (in one of which he succeeded, when
captured by Algerine pirates, in regaining
command of his ship without a struggle,
and in taking his revenge on his captors by
landing them in safety in their own country),
forms one of the most delightful narratives in
the Quaker literature.[1]

It was not until 1654 that any attempt
was made to preach the Quaker message in
London. Early in that year Isabel
1654 Buttery and another woman came
from the North and distributed in London a
number of printed epistles by George Fox.

They were joined by Amos Stoddart (who
had resigned his captain's commission in the
army on becoming a Quaker) and by one or
two others, and these were accustomed to
hold private meetings at the houses of the
brothers Dring in Watling Street and Moor-
fields, meetings held usually in silence, but
at which sometimes a few words would be
spoken by one of the women ministers.[2]

There was thus a little group of Friends
already accustomed to meet together for
worship and fellowship, when in the early

[1] Thomas Lurting, *The Fighting Sailor turn'd
peaceable Christian*, 1711, 8vo.

[2] W. Crouch, *Posthuma Christiana*, 1712, pp. 12, 13.

summer Francis Howgill and Edward Burrough, two of the most remarkable of the
early Quaker leaders, came to London in
company with Richard Hubberthorne and
several other Friends. One who was in
London at the time tells how "there was
a Report spread about the City that there
was a sort of people come there that went
by the name of plain North country plough-
men, who did differ in judgment to all other
people in the City," [1] and very soon they had
difficulty in finding rooms adequate to meet
the numbers that came to hear them, many
simply curious, others more deeply desirous
to seek the truth, wherever it might be found.
In the meantime, on their first arrival, the
Quaker preachers had paid repeated visits to
various religious groups which were likely to be
in sympathy with them. It was work which
needed tact and wisdom and deep spiritual
insight if the audience was to be reached.
"Much wisdom," writes Anthony Pearson
to George Fox (30th Fifth Month, 1654),
"is to be used amongst them until the truth
be clearly understood ; and then to speak to
that in their consciences, to the raising up of
the witness, to let them see themselves ; and
then to pass judgment upon them, and so to

[1] *First Publishers of Truth*, p. 163.

keep them under from disputing and questioning. This we found the most profitable
ministry; and few words must be used: for
they have the truth in notions, and all cry
out, 'What do these men say more than
others have said?'; but to bring them to
silence confounds their wisdom. Oh! that
none might come to London but those who
are raised up into the life of Truth, who dwell
in the loving power of God, whose words may
have authority; for there are so many mighty
in wisdom to oppose and gainsay, that weak
ones will suffer the Truth to be trampled on;
and there are so many rude, savage appren-
tices and young people and Ranters, that
nothing but the power of the Lord can chain
them. Dear heart, let none go to London
but in the clear and pure movings of the
Spirit of Life; that the blessing may rest
upon them. And great is the harvest like to
be in that city; hundreds are concerned, and
thousands wait to see the issue, who have
persuasion that it is the Truth. Very many
societies we have visited, and are now able to
stand: many honest hearts are among the
waiters, and some that are joined to the
Ranters are a pretty people." [1]

In a short time the little band of preachers

[1] *Letters, &c., of Early Friends*, 1841, p. 13.

separated to different parts of the country, with the exception of Howgill and Burrough, who still remained in the City. At the close of August, writing to Margaret Fell, they report that they "have three meetings or more every week, very large, more than any place will contain, and which we can conveniently meet in."[1] But to men so consumed with their message as were these, unexpected avenues of service were ever opening.

Such a scene as Sewel describes was but an instance of this. "At London there is a custom in summer time, when the evening approaches, and tradesmen leave off working, that many lusty fellows meet in the fields, to try their skill and strength in wrestling, when generally a multitude of people stands gazing in a round. Now it so fell out that E. Burrough past by the place when they were wrestling, and standing still among the spectators, saw how a strong and dexterous fellow had already thrown three others and was waiting for a fourth champion, if any durst venture into the lists. At length, none being bold enough to try, E. Burrough stept into the ring (commonly made up of all sorts of people) and having

[1] *Letters, &c., of Early Friends*, 1841, p. 16.

looked upon the wrestler with a serious
countenance, the man was not a little sur-
prised instead of an airy antagonist to meet
with a grave and awful young man ; and all
stood as it were amazed at this sight, eagerly
expecting what would be the issue of this
combat.   But it was quite another fight
E. Burrough aimed at.   For having already
fought against spiritual wickedness, that had
once prevailed on him, and having overcome
in measure, by the grace of God, he now
endeavoured also to fight against it in others,
and to turn them from the evil of their ways.
With this intention he began very seriously
to speak to the standers by, and that with
such a heart-piercing power, that he was
heard by this mixt multitude with no less
attention than admiration ; for his speech
tended to turn them from darkness to the
light, and from the power of Satan to
God." [1]

The work of Burrough and Howgill was
so effective that they were able in the same
year to leave London and pay a visit to
Ireland, where they spent some months,
visiting different parts of Munster, preaching
as they went, till after various adventures
they were arrested and brought under guard

[1] W. Sewel, *History*, ed. 1795, vol. i. pp. 149, 150.

from Cork to Dublin, to be banished the country.[1]

From this time onwards there was very close intercourse between the Friends in England and their Irish comrades, and the development of the Society proceeded upon similar lines in both countries. The Irish Friends were almost entirely recruited from the Protestant settlers, so that difference of nationality did not so much affect the growth of the Quaker organisation as might otherwise have been the case.

Burrough and Howgill were banished from Ireland, but they had left an impression on the English settlers there which other preachers were not slow to follow up; indeed, on the very day on which they were banished

[1] The Quaker message was first brought to Ireland in 1653 by William Edmundson, who had been convinced by George Fox in the North of England in that year, and subsequently went to join his brother, a Cromwellian soldier, quartered in Antrim. He moved soon afterwards to Lurgan, where the first Friends' meeting was established, but his public ministry did not begin until 1655, when he began to travel about in company with an English Friend, John Tiffin, and from that time onward led a life of most useful service, both in different parts of Ireland and in England, America, and the West Indies. See his Journal (Dublin, 1715, 4to).

Barbara Blaugdon, a woman of great courage,
with remarkable gifts as a minister, landed in
Dublin and, after an interview with Henry
Cromwell, travelled through the South of
Ireland to Cork, holding meetings and suffering repeated imprisonments. In the meantime the two friends returned to London,
which for the remainder of their lives became
the centre of their labours. Edward Burrough indeed went on missionary visits to
Scotland, Dunkirk, and elsewhere, but for
both the absorbing work of their lives lay
henceforth in London and its immediate
neighbourhood.

Within about six months of their first
arrival in London the numbers of their
friends had so grown that they were able
to arrange to rent a large meeting-house at
the sign of the "Bull and Mouth" in Alders-
gate Street for public gatherings, while small
private meetings were held in some thirty
houses. At first the work of organisation
must have lain heavily upon them, but after
some two years' time, as Burrough wrote to
George Fox, he and Francis Howgill were
"wholly given up to the work of the
ministry," and the needful organisation and
care of the poor was undertaken by a
fortnightly meeting of the more experienced

men Friends, from which none who cared to attend were excluded.[1]

Those who would gather some idea of the growth of the Quaker Society in London in these early days will find a lively picture from the pen of an eye-witness in the *Posthuma Christiana* of William Crouch. He speaks of Burrough and Howgill as "the apostles of this city in their day," and bears strong witness to the peculiar power of Edward Burrough as a minister. "At the 'Bull and Mouth,' when the room, which was very large, hath been filled with people, many of whom have been in uproar, contending with one another, some exclaiming against the Quakers, accusing and charging them with heresie, blasphemy, sedition, and what not, that they were deceivers and deluded the people, that they denied the Holy Scriptures and the Resurrection, others endeavouring to vindicate them and speaking of them more favourably, in the midst of all which noise and contention this servant of

[1] See W. Beck and T. F. Ball, *The London Friends' Meetings*, 1869, 8vo, p. 24 and p. 85 *seq.* The "Two Weeks' Meeting" continued to exist until 1789 for the care of marriages, but its other duties were undertaken from 1671 onwards by the Monthly Meeting.

the Lord hath stood upon a bench with his
Bible in his hand—for he generally carried
one about with him—speaking to the people
with great authority from the words of John
vii. 12: 'And there was much murmuring
among the people concerning Him' (to wit,
Jesus), 'for some said, He is a good man :
others said, Nay, but He deceiveth the
people.' And so suitable to the present
debate amongst them, that the whole multitude were overcome thereby and became
exceeding calm and attentive, and departed
peaceably, and with seeming satisfaction." [1]

The power of Edward Burrough was that
of a nature intensely religious and of a life
wholly given up to the service to which he
believed himself called of God. In the
interesting preface which he wrote to George
Fox's *Great Mystery . . . Unfolded* he alludes
with simple modesty to his own experience
as one of those who from the strictest
Puritanism had turned to Quakerism. "Such
we were (to say no more of us) that
sought the Lord, and desired the knowledge of His ways more than anything
beside, and for one I may speak, who from
a child even a few years old, he set his face
to seek and find the Saviour, and more than

[1] *Posthuma Christiana*, p. 26 *seq.*

life and treasure, or any mortal crown sought after with all his heart the one thing that is needful, to wit, the knowledge of God."

Of such a spirit was Edward Burrough, a man, as his friend Howgill wrote, whose "very strength was bended after God," and to whose attractive power the Journal of Thomas Ellwood still bears witness. His life of service was fittingly crowned by its close, which was indeed a martyr's death. It was after the Restoration and in the first flush of persecution which succeeded the brief interval of half-hearted toleration that he learned when in Bristol that the storm had broken upon his beloved Friends. " I am going up to the City of London," he said, "to suffer among Friends in that place."

Soon after his return he was arrested at the " Bull and Mouth " meeting and condemned by the Lord Mayor, Sir Richard Brown, to Newgate. The jails of London were filled with Quakers, and Newgate was so crowded that there was not room for many of the Friends to sleep upon the ground. Rough usage and foul air soon told and one after another sickened and died. When after some four months Edward Burrough fell ill a special effort was made to obtain his removal from the dungeon, and an

1662

order for his release was obtained from the King, but Brown was determined not to let his prisoner go, and put obstacles in the way. As Burrough lay dying he prayed for his persecutor, and on the morning before his death he is recorded to have said, "Now my soul and spirit is centred into its own being with God, and this form of person must return from whence it was taken."[1] He was but twenty-eight years of age at his death, but so deeply did his whole life impress his friends that when in 1666 they collected and published his writings the title-page spoke of him as "that true prophet and faithful servant of God."

[1] J. Besse, *Sufferings*, 1753, 4to, vol. i. p. 389, and *cf. Piety Promoted*, vol. i. p. 56.

V

TROUBLES WITHOUT AND WITHIN

WE have seen how, in 1652, George Fox had found at Swarthmore a centre for his work, and in the two succeeding years he journeyed up and down in the North-west of England, intent upon his message. At Ulverstone, and again at Walney Island, he was clubbed and stoned and knocked senseless by the crowd; in Cumberland he found in many places an eager reception for his words.

But at Carlisle, where the garrison had assembled with beat of drum to hear him preach, there was sharp division of feeling amongst the townspeople about him, and after a scene of confusion in one of the churches a warrant was issued against him. Hearing of this, Fox delivered himself up to the magistrates, and was committed to prison for blasphemy and heresy. He was threatened with death, but some technical difficulty stood in the way of his being tried at the Assizes, and the judges left him to the local magistrates to deal with. He was put by them, without trial, into the common dungeon, " among the moss-troopers, thieves, and murderers "—a verminous and filthy place, where Fox was kept for months, 1653-54 ill-used by the jailers, but beloved by his fellow-prisoners. Among those who came to see the man who, as it was rumoured, was to be put to death for his belief, was a lad of sixteen, James Parnell by name. He was convinced of the truth of the cause for which the prisoner was suffering, and became in turn one of its earliest martyrs. His parents were people of means, who had given him a good education, but on his returning home to Retford as a Quaker he was disowned by them. But though small of stature and so young in years, Parnell seems to have had remarkable gifts as a minister, and courage undaunted. Leaving his friends, he went forth as a Quaker preacher to bear the brunt of the persecution which was now growing with the increasing prejudice aroused by the new teaching.

In Huntingdonshire, at Cambridge (where

he disputed with the scholars, and was imprisoned), and in Essex, he was the first to
bring the Quaker message, and in the latter
county he was the means of convincing a
very large number, among them Stephen
Crisp, of Colchester, who afterwards became
one of the most eminent of Quaker ministers.

Meanwhile opposition to the heresy increased. Parnell had often to suffer for the
part he played, though his gentle spirit is
witnessed by the way in which he bore persecution. As he came out of St. Nicholas's
Church, Colchester, a man struck him a
fierce blow with a heavy stick, saying,
"There, take that for Christ's sake!" to
which he quietly answered, "Friend, I do
receive it for Jesus Christ's sake." [1] In the
summer of 1655 the Independents at Cogge-
shall had appointed a fast "to pray against
the errors of the people called Quakers," in

1655 the parish church. Parnell went
there, and on the conclusion of
the minister's sermon spoke on behalf of the
heretics. Various ministers argued with him,
and one, after accusing him of falsehood and
slander, went on, without leaving an opportunity for reply, to offer up a prayer. Upon
this Parnell did not remove his hat (which it

[1] Sewel, vol. i. p. 196.

was customary then to wear in church ex-
cept during vocal prayer), and when the
magistrates bade him put it off he refused,
and went out of the church. One of the
magistrates presently followed him, and he
was committed to the common jail at Colchester, and eventually taken, as one of a
chained gang of felons, to the Assizes at
Chelmsford. The jury were unwilling to find
him guilty of anything but the authorship of
a paper in which he had answered his mitti-
mus, but the judge was determined that he
should be made an example of, and fined
him £40 "for contempt of the magistracy
and ministry." He was sent back to prison
in Colchester Castle, where his friends were
forbidden access to him. The jailer and his
wife used to beat him, he was robbed of the
food his friends brought, and forced to lie on
the cold stones, instead of on the bed which
they would have provided for him. At
length he was compelled to live in a hole in
the wall some twelve feet above the ground.
His friends wished to provide a cord and
basket, by which he might draw up his food,
but the jailer would not permit it, and he
had to clamber down the wall by the aid of
a rope to the ladder, which only reached half
the distance. He grew stiff and weak from

living in this damp cell, and one day as he tried to climb back with his food, and clutched at the rope, he slipped and fell, bruising himself and cutting his head severely upon the stones beneath. He was taken up for dead, but on his coming round he was forced into another hole in the wall, lower down than the first and smaller, known as "the Oven." It had a door but no windows, and they would not let him leave it to take a little air, or even permit him exercise in the prison yard. Friends who offered bail for him and were willing to be imprisoned in his stead until he should recover, were refused their request by the magistrate; but as the prisoner drew near his end, after an imprisonment of some ten or eleven months, one or two Quakers were allowed to visit him. He himself looked gladly forward to death. "Don't hold me, but let me go," he said. "Will you hold me?" "No, dear heart, we will not hold thee," was the rejoinder of the good woman Friend who, with her husband, was watching beside him; and after a little slumber death set him free.

In the meantime the imprisonment of Fox in Carlisle Jail had come to an end. It was reported to Parliament (the famous "Little Parliament" of Praisegod Barebones) "that a

8

young man at Carlisle was to die for religion," [1] and in consequence apparently of its
action in communicating with the magistrates and sheriffs Fox was shortly afterwards released, and at once continued his
work of preaching, travelling through Durham, Northumberland, and Yorkshire.   In
1654 he revisited his own country in the
Midlands, and at Swannington, in Leicestershire, a "general meeting" was held, to
which the leading Quaker preachers from
Bristol, London, and other parts also came.

The attention of the authorities must have
been drawn to this gathering as proof of
some sort of national organisation
amongst these Quakers, of whom
so much ill was spoken, and not long afterwards Fox was arrested by Colonel Hacker,
the regicide, and sent up in charge of one
of his captains to London to the Protector,
under suspicion of being concerned in a
Royalist plot.

It was no difficult thing for Fox to show to
Cromwell that his aim was to bring people
"from the causes of war and fighting," and
that he was opposed to taking up arms either
against the Protector or any other man.   As
Fox turned to leave Oliver's presence, he

1654

[1] Journal, i. p. 174.

caught him by the hand and said, with tears in his eyes, "Come again to my house, for if thou and I were but an hour a day together, we should be nearer one to the other."[1] The Quaker leader left Whitehall a free man once more, but though Cromwell himself was inclined towards toleration, the temper of the party upon whose support his Government relied was very different, and the persecution still went on, the Presbyterian and independent clergy being annoyed not only by the doctrines of Quakerism, but also by the sturdy refusal of the Friends to contribute by payment of tithes towards the compulsory maintenance of a professional ministry. After travelling through the Eastern Counties, and the Western Midlands, Fox had passed into Cornwall, and at St. Ives he was arrested and taken to Launceston, where, at the Assizes, his captor, Major Ceely, accused him of a plot to bring in King Charles by force of arms. The charge utterly broke down, but Fox and his two companions were fined twenty marks each for not removing their hats in court, and sentenced to be kept in prison until the fine should be paid.

As they had now to prepare for a long

[1] Journal, i. p. 211.

imprisonment they discontinued the fees for maintenance which they had been giving to the jailer, and in consequence were thrust into the loathsome dungeon of "Doomsdale," where the condemned murderers were kept, and many prisoners had died—a place so foul and unhealthy that it was said that "few that went in ever came out again in health." After some considerable time, the prisoners were allowed by Quarter Sessions to cleanse their dungeon, which had not been done for many years. While they continued in prison their teaching continued to spread, and the magistrates of the Exeter Quarter Sessions were induced to issue a warrant for apprehending all Quakers, and many other Friends were arrested and imprisoned. But in the meantime protests and appeals had been made to the Protector, and Major-General Desborough was ordered to release the prisoners at Launceston. In the early autumn they were set free again, after more than half a year's imprisonment, and Fox was able to continue his travels. But there lay before him a trouble greater than that of persecution, a moment of crisis for the new movement which was to have the most far-reaching effect upon its inner life.

1656

There can be no doubt that wave of intense enthusiasm which spread over the country with the teaching of the first Quaker preachers carried with it a number of minds naturally susceptible to excitement and liable to strange and one-sided conceptions of truth and duty. Here and there a Quaker would follow the example of one of the old Hebrew prophets to call attention to his message : there are a number of cases in which preachers appeared in sackcloth or in a penance sheet of white, and even one or two in which they appeared stript, or almost stript, of their clothing, "for a sign" to the people. Such acts, though they gave offence, may be paralleled by similar ones in the case of other great religious movements, and may, to some extent, be explained by the way in which the thoughts and imagery of the Old Testament writers reacted upon the men of Puritan England. But incidents like these, although they were the outcome of Quaker enthusiasm, were after all external to the real life of the movement, and became rarer as it gathered strength. The danger which Fox had now to face lay deeper, and one who had been most closely associated with him in his work hitherto was to be connected with it. James Nayler was one of the most remarkable

of the yeomen preachers who followed the
example of Fox and gave themselves up
without reserve to an arduous life of travelling
ministry. Almost since the year of his
convincement in 1651, Nayler had left his
wife and family at Wakefield to travel about
as a Quaker preacher, at first in the North,
and later in the South and West. A man of
no great education, looking, as Ellwood tells
us, "but like a plain, simple countryman,
having the appearance of a husbandman or
shepherd,"[1] he possessed considerable natural
abilities, and had risen, while serving with the
army, to be quartermaster under General
Lambert, who bore witness in Parliament to
the honourable position which he filled, until,
in consequence of ill-health, he left the army.
His decision to follow the example of Fox
involved him in excommunication, and en-
tailed a life of continual hardships. He suffered
beatings and imprisonment, and, like Fox,
employed his moments of leisure in writing
pamphlets full of burning enthusiasm for the
cause of Quakerism. He possessed, too, a
personal charm which strongly attracted
many to him, and this was, perhaps,
heightened by an ascetic tendency which led
him to undergo prolonged fastings which left

[1] *The History of Thomas Ellwood*, edn. 1900, p. 13.

him weak in body and liable to nervous excitement. Unfortunately he was not equally proof against the admiration which his great powers aroused amongst many of his hearers.

The first sign of any difficulty arose not long after the coming of the northern preachers to London. Amid the multitude of new converts there were some whose spirit and ideas were really those of the Ranters, enthusiasts eager to dispute, and carried away by their imagination. Among them were some women, who troubled the Friends' meetings by disputes with Burrough and Howgill, and who appealed from their rebukes to Nayler. His kindness of heart, perhaps, led him astray into giving them some tacit support, and eventually a group of these people gathered about him, flattering him by their admiration of his power as a preacher and gradually bringing about a silent estrangement between him and his fellow-workers. It was under these influences that the very truth which Nayler had been so long proclaiming began to be distorted in his followers' minds into a grievous error. Conscious of the reality of the presence of the Divine revelation, the indwelling Christ, in his heart, he seems to have lacked that personal humility which with Fox and the other Quaker leaders prevented them from claiming any place of privilege apart from other men. He allowed his followers to do honour to him under the supposition that they were honouring not himself but the Spirit of Christ revealed in him. His friends in prison learned with deep sadness of the way in which Nayler allowed this delusion place, permitting his followers to bow and even kneel to him.

On his journey back from Launceston, George Fox came upon Nayler and his company imprisoned in Exeter Jail. He endeavoured in vain to convince them of their error, and held a meeting with them in the prison, but they were not able to stay through this ordeal. Next day Fox spoke earnestly to his former comrade, but all without avail, and he had to turn from his proffered kiss of friendship, "since he had turned, against the power of God." [1]

When they were released shortly afterwards from prison, Nayler and six of his followers went to Bristol. On the way his companions imitated the behaviour of Christ's disciples at His triumphant entry into Jerusalem, throwing their scarfs in front of him

[1] Journal, i. p. 328.

and singing as they went. It was raining and
the streets lay deep in mud as they entered
Bristol, a man walking in front bareheaded,
and Nayler following on horseback, with
women walking beside him singing, " Holy,
holy, holy, is the Lord God of hosts,
Hosannah in the highest." The strange
scene did not pass unobserved, and the
magistrates promptly arrested the misguided
folk, and sent them up to London to be tried

1656 by Parliament, which had but
recently met. A committee of
the House of Commons took many days to
examine Nayler, and the House itself debated
his case at great length.

In reply to the question, " Art thou the
only Son of God?" he said, " I am the Son
of God, but I have many brethren," and at
the close, " I do abhor that any of that honour
which is due to God, should be given to me,
as I am a creature ; but it pleased the Lord
to set me up as a sign of the coming of the
Righteous One. . . ." Apparently even under
the cloud which rested over him he had never
identified himself with Christ. After a dozen
discussions the House at last found him
" guilty of horrid blasphemy," and " a grand
impostor and seducer of the people." Barely
escaping sentence of death, he was condemned

to be twice pilloried, to be whipped through
the streets of London, bored through the
tongue with a hot iron, and branded on the
forehead with the letter B.   Then after a
public exposure and whipping at Bristol, he
was to be imprisoned during the pleasure of
Parliament.   The cruel sentence, against
which Cromwell expressed to the House his
strong disapproval, was carried out remorse-
lessly, in spite of a public petition and other
expressions of popular protest. The occasion
was eagerly seized by many of the Puritan
leaders to make a general attack upon the
Quakers, who, in spite of their having
expressed their strong disapproval of Nayler
and his companions long before this, were
readily identified with them by their opponents.   The Swarthmore MSS. contain copies
of letters written by Fox to Nayler previous
to his arrest, which show how completely he
realised the serious nature of his conduct,
both in itself and in its effect on public
opinion.[1]

[1] "James, thou must bear thy own burden and thy
company's with thee, whose iniquity doth increase,
and by thee is not cried against.   Thou hast satisfied
the world, yea their desires which they looked for,
thou and thy disciples, and the world is joined
against the truth : it is manifest through your wilful-

During the years of his imprisonment
Nayler at length returned to his right mind
completely, and wrote an earnest and
humble acknowledgment of his error and of
his gratitude to the Divine love which had
compassion upon him. He was supported
through his terrible punishment by the
sympathy and care of not a few of his former
Quaker friends, and now in his penitence
there were two especially to whom his
thoughts turned in his desire for full unity
with his old companions. In 1658 we find
him writing · to Margaret Fell : " Dear
Sister, beloved of God, I am often with thee,
and have seen thee as thou art to mewards,
and have heard thy voice as if present with
thee, and sometimes have been refreshed
therewith in the time of heavy burthens
. . . but truly for the hardness and irrecon-

ness and stubbornness, and this is the word of the
Lord God to thee."

[From a letter found upon Nayler when he was
examined.]

" And James, it will be harder for thee to get
down thy rude company than it was for thee to set
them up (if ever thou come to know and own
Christ) whose impudence doth sport and blaspheme
the truth.' *

_____

* Swarthmore MSS., $\frac{3}{193}$, $\frac{3}{195}$.

cileableness which is in some, I am astonished and shaken, lest the Spirit of Christ Jesus should be grieved and depart, for if I know anything of it or ever have done, that is it which naturall[y] inclines to mercy and forgiveness, and not to bind one another under a trespass till the uttermost farthen ; though this may be just and I do not condemn it, yet I have felt a spirit which delights more in forgiving debts and seeks all occasion thereto, even where it is not sought to, but seeks ; and by this spirit I have been able to bear all things while it is with me, else had I not been at this day. So that I complain not as to myself in what I here write, God knows, but *my* fear is of the provoking the justice of God without mercy, through not showing mercy one to another. . . . Dear friend, thou mayest feel my heart by what I have written to thee, which I fear to do to others. . . . So to the wisdom of Christ Jesus I commit thee therein, whose Spirit is simple and harmless toward fools and babes." [1]

We can well imagine how Margaret Fell would do her best to bridge the gulf between Nayler and her friends. And in this work of reconciliation a most helpful part was borne by William Dewsbury, perhaps the most

[1] Swarthmore MSS.

lovable of all the early Quaker leaders in his
complete unselfishness and gentleness of
spirit. Dewsbury seems to have come up to
London in obedience to a deep sense of duty,
and to have laboured earnestly to bring back
those who had followed Nayler in the time
of his aberration. To Nayler himself he
wrote a letter of the kindliest counsel and
admonition, in which he showed to him his
responsibility for the error of his followers.
Finally, ere he left London, Dewsbury was
able to bring about a meeting and complete
reconciliation between George Fox, Burrough,
and Howgill, and their old friend.[1]

The closing years of James Nayler's life
were spent in complete unison with his
fellows, and the terrible experience through
which he had passed seems to have left
behind it no trace of bitterness towards his
enemies. In his suffering he had learned a
great lesson, and henceforward gentleness
and humility characterised his whole life.
He was finally released from Bridewell by
Parliament, in September, 1659, and proceeded
to Bristol, where his public confession of his
error and earnest appeal to his hearers
brought tears to the listeners' eyes.

[1] Edward Smith, *The Life of William Dewsbury*,
1836, 8vo, pp. 145–148.

danger of individual liberty being turned to wild and unbalanced licence. He was no theologian, and when he wished to remove the false impressions of his aims which were spread abroad by his opponents long after the death of Nayler, he expressed his consciousness of unity with historic Christianity in language not unlike that of the creeds of the orthodox Churches. At various times before the close of the seventeenth century the Friends found it desirable to remove misconceptions by publishing similar declarations of their belief, though these never took the form of a creed to which every member of their Society was expected to subscribe. Probably the best known of these expressions of belief is the letter of George Fox to the Governor of Barbadoes, written in 1671 and frequently reprinted.

Such writings contain an expression of truths of vital importance, yet they represent very imperfectly what was the real strength of the Quaker movement. Fox was not a methodical thinker, but he was a man whose whole life was dominated by his vision of the Unseen, and controlled by his conviction of a real communion between the human and the Divine. This was an experience and a faith which his fellow-preachers shared and which made the early Quakers what they were.

VI

THE CROWN OF PERSECUTION

WHEN Cromwell's second Parliament passed its cruel sentence upon James Nayler the door was opened to a general outburst of persecution against the Quakers; country members appealed to the House of Commons to frame some measure against this dangerous and seditious sect, and magistrates and judges vied in their zeal to make examples of the troublesome heretics. Some were punished for breaking the Sabbath, others for non-payment of tithes; often a refusal to take off the hat was treated as contempt of court, and the law against vagrants was applied with vigour to travelling preachers. Thus, in spite of the limited toleration which was proclaimed by Cromwell's Instrument of Government, there were at one time over a thousand Quakers in prison under his rule. Fox, Burrough,

9

Thomas Aldam and other Friends on more than one occasion endeavoured to lay before the Protector the iniquity of this persecution, but without effecting any permanent change of policy. Although during the three last years of the Commonwealth Fox was able to travel about preaching in Wales and in Scotland without suffering the hardships he underwent in his earlier journeys, there were still many Friends in prison, and petition was made to Parliament in 1659 for

1659   the release of 144 such sufferers for conscience sake, but in vain. Strong, however, as was the opposition to the Quakers amongst the Puritans in Britain, it was in New England that the spirit of intolerance found fullest expression. The successors of the Pilgrim Fathers had forgotten all too soon the beautiful parting sermon that John Robinson addressed to his people at Leiden ere they set sail for America. Already Roger Williams had been rewarded by banishment for his tolerant spirit, which had led him to protest against the law by which all colonists were compelled to attend public worship on Sundays, and in 1637 Anne Hutchinson and her followers were exiled from Massachusetts. Subsequently, too, numbers of Anabaptists were punished by the colonists by whippings and banishment. The law confined the franchise to members of the Independent Churches, and every endeavour was made by ministers and magistrates to guard the privileges which they had left their English homes to gain. Thus it may be imagined that no kindly welcome awaited the arrival of the first Quaker preachers in New England, especially since these were two women—Mary Fisher and Anne Austin.

1656 On their reaching Boston they were detained on shipboard by order of the Deputy-Governor and their luggage was searched. A large number of Quaker books were taken from them and burned by the common executioner, they themselves were stripped and examined to see if marks of witchcraft could be found upon them, and finally, after some five weeks in jail, were banished by order of the Council to Barbadoes.

Shortly after their deportation another ship arrived in Boston harbour bringing eight other Quaker missionaries. Their chests were promptly searched for " erroneous books and hellish pamphlets," and the men and women brought before the court, which was then in session. After two days' examination, sentence of banishment was pronounced

against them, and their ship's captain was
compelled to take them back to England.
The Boston authorities were now thoroughly
alarmed, and, after consultation with the
Commissioners of the United Provinces, a law
was passed enforcing a penalty of £100 upon
any ship's master who knowingly brought in
any Quaker; such Quakers, after being
whipped and imprisoned with hard labour,
were to be deported at the earliest opportunity. Fines were also to be levied on any
who concealed or dispersed Quaker books
or defended their opinions.

The law was publicly proclaimed by beat
of drum in the streets of Boston. A kindly
disposed citizen, Nicholas Upshall, who
(though not permitted by the jailer to speak
to the prisoners) had previously furnished
Mary Fisher and Anne Austin with food
while they lay in prison, was summoned to
appear before the court "for having expressed his disapproval of the law against
Quakers." He appeared before the magistrates and pleaded with them against their
intolerance, but the only result was that they
sentenced the old man to a fine of £20, and
banishment within thirty days.

In the following year the authorities were
equally merciless to two women who landed

at Boston, with no intention of preaching: one of them, Ann Burden, a poor widow who came to collect some debts due to her husband; the other, Mary Dyer, returning from a journey to England to rejoin her husband in Long Island.

In the meantime Christopher Holder and five of the eight Friends already banished from Boston felt that it was still their duty to return and fulfil their message, and they were joined by five other Quaker ministers. There seemed, however, to be no way open by which they could reach their destination, in view of the heavy fine which any captain would incur who ventured to take them with him.

While they were in this difficulty there came to London a little craft, whose builder and owner was Robert Fowler, a Quaker minister of Bridlington. While building his ship he had felt that she was to have some special service, and on reaching London he came to open his heart on the matter to Gerard Roberts.

Robert Fowler had no experience of ocean navigation, and his vessel was a very small one, but it seemed clear that the opportunity they had desired was come, and the ten Quakers started on their perilous journey. The master's account of the voyage is still preserved,[1] telling how the little ship *Woodhouse* crossed the Atlantic without the usual aids of navigation, amid dangers of capture from hostile cruisers and of wreckage upon unknown rocks. At times of doubt and difficulty the little band would meet together for worship, and the ship was steered in accordance with what was felt to be the Divine guidance, "regarding neither latitude nor longitude," until they came safely to land at Long Island, the very place which some of the travellers had felt drawn to visit. At New Amsterdam, after two months' voyage, the travellers divided into two parties, and presently separated over different parts of the country.

1657

Mary Clark reached Boston alone, and there she was cruelly whipped and kept for three months in jail. Christopher Holder and John Copeland were banished from Martha's Vineyard (where the Indians, however, gave them welcome) and from Plymouth, and after being whipped in Boston till their flesh was all torn, they were left for three days in prison without food or drink. Presently another Friend shared

[1] MS. at Devonshire House, printed in J. Bowden's *History of the Society of Friends in America,* 1850, vol. i. p. 63, *seq.*

their fate, and the Governor ordered them "to be severely whipped twice a week," the number of lashes to be increased from fifteen by three lashes each time. A new law was passed to deal with Quakers who should return after banishment, prescribing ear-clipping, whipping, and finally boring of the tongue, in punishment for this offence. Popular sympathy, however, had now been aroused on behalf of the prisoners, in consequence of their repeated whippings, and they were discharged and banished.

Up and down New England the Quakers passed, and they and their converts were stripped and lashed in public and banished from place after place. Travelling was dangerous, and three ministers lost their lives by shipwreck; three of those who had returned to Boston, after having been condemned and scourged, had their right ears cut off, and were refused appeal to England. Only in Rhode Island and among the Indians on the mainland was there security for the hated heretics.

At length, in the autumn of 1658, upon a petition of the ministers, the legislature of Massachusetts passed (by a majority of one) a law to enable "every person or persons of the cursed sect of Quakers" not an inhabi-

tant of the jurisdiction to be apprehended
without warrant, and after trial and conviction to be banished upon pain of death.
Colonists were to be allowed a month's
imprisonment, during which they might
recant, and were then to incur the same
penalty. In 1659 came the additional
enactment that "all children and servants
and others that for conscience sake cannot
come to their meetings to worship, and have
not estates in their hands to answer the fines,
must be sold for slaves to Barbadoes or
Virginia, or other remote parts." [1]

In spite of all persecution, however, the
magistrates could not prevent the spread of
the new movement, and from time to time
Friends from England succeeded in entering
the forbidden country. In 1659 the climax
came. In this year William Robinson, one
of the ten who came on the *Woodhouse*, and
whose work hitherto had lain in Virginia,
came to Rhode Island, where he met
Marmaduke Stevenson and another Quaker
who had recently landed from Barbadoes.
There he learned of the persecution of
Friends in Massachusetts. He was deeply
stirred by the news, and, as he afterwards
wrote to the magistrates before his execu-

[1] Bowden, vol. i. p. 165.

tion, one afternoon, while he was walking from Newport, "the word of the Lord came expressly to me, filling me with life and power and heavenly love," constraining him to pass to the town of Boston, " my life to lay down in His will for the accomplishing of His service, . . . to which heavenly voice I presently yielded obedience, not questioning the Lord how He would bring the thing to pass, being [as] I was a child ; and obedience was demanded of me by the Lord, who filled me with living strength and power from His heavenly presence, which at that time did mightily overshadow me, and my life at that time did say Amen to what the Lord required of me, and had commanded me to do."[1]

Marmaduke Stevenson, who had left behind him in the East Riding a wife and children whom he dearly loved, felt that it was his duty to go with his friend and share his message and punishment. The two landed at Boston on a fast-day, and after the minister had ended his sermon they attempted to speak to the congregation, and were promptly committed to prison, along with two other Quakers, one of whom was Patience Scott, a child of eleven years, who had come some

[1] *Piety Promoted*, 1723, pt. i. p. 13, *seq.*

weeks before from Rhode Island to plead
with the Boston zealots. They were presently joined by a fellow-prisoner, Mary
Dyer, who had come from Rhode Island
to visit and comfort them. All but the
little child were sentenced by the court to
banishment on pain of death, if they should
be found within the jurisdiction after two
days from their release.

Undeterred by this sentence, Robinson and
Stevenson went out to Salem and held great
meetings in the woods, since none dare receive them into their houses. Mary Dyer
went back to Rhode Island, but not long
afterwards felt it her duty to return to
Boston. She visited some Friends who were
in prison there, and shortly afterwards was
arrested. A few days later Robinson and
Stevenson, having finished the work which
they felt they had to do in the country,
entered Boston again. The undaunted men
were accompanied by a little group of
Quakers, men and women, one of whom
brought with her linen, "to wrap the dead
bodies of those who were to suffer." News
of their approach had gone before them, and
they were met by the constables and by a
mocking crowd, taken before the magistrates,
and committed again to jail.

At length the court met. The prisoners had broken the law, but even Endicott seems **1659** to have hesitated before pronouncing sentence ; but on the prisoners being remanded for a day, a fierce sermon was delivered by the minister whose duty it was to preach on the occasion of the public fast which fell then, urging the magistrates to remove the curse of the Quakers' presence from their country. The Governor's mind was now fixed, and the prisoners being brought into court again, he proceeded at once to pass sentence of death upon William Robinson, not even permitting him to read a paper he had prepared, giving the reasons which had led him to remain in the colony. Marmaduke Stevenson was sentenced next, and finally Mary Dyer. In the interval before the execution William Robinson preached through the prison window to the crowd which had flocked together. After another service, when the minister once more attacked the diabolical doctrines of the Quakers, an escort of two hundred soldiers took the prisoners out to the place where the gibbet stood. To prevent the people from hearing what they might say, the drums were beaten loudly close beside them. The three walked hand in hand, their faces full of joy. Mary Dyer was an elderly woman, and the marshal scoffingly asked her whether she was not ashamed to walk thus hand in hand between two young men. "No," she made answer, "this is to me the greatest joy I could enjoy in this world." The two men spoke briefly to the people before they were hanged, and, despite the taunts of Wilson, the attendant minister, they died calmly and full of faith. As Mary Dyer stood bound and blindfolded upon the ladder, with the halter on her neck, a shout was raised that a reprieve had come, and she was taken down. Her son had suceeded in interceding for her.

They bade her come down, but she, as Sewel says, "whose mind was already in heaven, stood still, and said she was there willing to suffer as her brethren did, unless they would annul their wicked law." Then the officers pulled her down, and removed her to prison, whence she was before long carried under escort out of Boston. Robinson had left behind him two letters written shortly before his execution, filled with a wonderful joy and calm, and more than one of the spectators of the event were so impressed that they were willing to suffer the lash for siding with the Quakers.

Mary Dyer did not stay long in her home, but in the spring of 1660 felt it her duty to return and renew her protest. She was once more condemned, and this time the sentence was duly carried out, in spite of a most touching appeal to Endicott from her husband, who was a leading man in Rhode Island and not a Quaker. As she was about to suffer, one scoffingly said to her that she should have said she had been in paradise. "Yea, I have been in paradise these several days," she answered, and then the executioner did his work.

In the following year William Leddra was hanged, dying with a like calmness of faith. A fourth Quaker was about to **1661** suffer, and many others were in prison when Endicott's hand was suddenly stayed by an order from Charles II. The first year of the Restoration was a time in which great expectations of toleration were general. The Act of Uniformity had not yet been passed, and men still had faith in the Declaration of Breda. When Edward Burrough went to lay before the king the sufferings of the New England Quakers, the good-natured monarch doubtless smiled as he consented to make one Samuel Shattock, a Quaker whom Endicott had already exiled, his messenger to the Puritan Governor, bearing the royal mandamus that "now and henceforth all Quakers liable to death or other corporal punishment" should be sent to England for trial. Henceforth, though persecution in America was still anything but ended, the worst was passed, and it was in England that the Quakers were now to suffer in the largest numbers.

The toleration which Charles had promised did not last long. The rising of
1661 Venner and the Fifth Monarchy men in January, 1660–1, was made an excuse for a proclamation by which Anabaptists and Quakers, who were in no way connected with the Fifth Monarchists, were forbidden to meet together for worship, save in their own families or in the parish church. This was followed in May, 1662, by a special act against the Quakers, providing that all who maintained the unlawfulness of oaths, and all Quakers meeting for worship to the number of five or more, should be fined £5
1662 for the first offence, £10 for the second, and for the third be banished to the Plantations, with alternatives of three or six months' hard labour in place of the fines. The final punishment was thus even more severe than that to

which all Dissenters were subjected for a
like offence on the passing of the Conventicle
Act in 1664, for by that Act a fine of £100
was allowed as the alternative to transportation for seven years. In addition to these
Acts advantage was taken of the cruel penal
laws of Elizabeth and James I., which had
been aimed originally against the Roman
Catholics. Especially was this the case with
the Act of 1605, under which Quakers refusing the oath of allegiance at quarter
sessions now ran risk of a præmunire, by
which they were outlawed and subject to
perpetual imprisonment at the pleasure of
the Crown, with loss of all their goods.
Finally, in 1670, the Second Conventicle Act
made the penalties against the meetings of
Dissenters more stringent, in some respects,
even than those of the Acts of 1664.

Soon after the Restoration, George Fox
suffered imprisonment for some five months
at Lancaster, from which he was freed
through the intercession of Judge Fell's
widow with the king, but it was in 1662 that
the full brunt of persecution fell upon the
Quakers, to continue, with but a few intervals
of comparative relaxation, until the close of
the reign of Charles II. Thomas Ellwood
has vividly portrayed the terrible overcrowd-

ing of the prisoners in Newgate,[1] where in one room three tiers of hammocks were stretched one above the other from the centre pillar to the walls, while the sick and dying lay on pallet beds beneath. Twenty of the Newgate prisoners died in consequence of this treatment, and throughout the country the jails were crowded with Quakers. While under the Commonwealth 3,173 Friends had been put in prison, of whom 32 had died there, as many as 3,068 had been imprisoned in less than two years after the Restoration. We learn these details from a letter which Fox wrote to the king, pointing out how, in addition to these sufferings, the meetings of the Quakers were " daily broken up by men with clubs and arms."[2]

One after another the Quaker leaders of the early days were taken from their work by the zeal of the authorities. Hubberthorne and Burrough had died in Newgate in 1662 ; Francis Howgill, after an imprisonment of four and a half years for refusal to take the oath of allegiance, died in peace in Appleby Jail in 1668. Fox himself suffered, under circumstances of great hardship, prolonged

---

[1] *The History of the Life of Thomas Ellwood*, 1900, 8vo, p. 107, *seq*.

[2] Journal, i. p. 522.

imprisonment, first at Lancaster in 1663, and then at Scarborough Castle, to which he had been transferred under escort. Here he was exposed to the weather and the spray of the waves, in a cheerless cell by the edge of the cliff, until, though his health was shattered by the repeated hardships of imprisonment, the very soldiers who had taken pleasure in trying to annoy him could not but express their wonder at his spirit ("he is as stiff as a tree and as pure as a bell, for we could never bow him," they said), and at length even the Roman Catholic Governor was won over from hostility to lifelong friendliness.

It is hardly possible, however, in recording some of the punishments which the Quaker leaders underwent, to realise the severity of the persecution through which a countless number of obscure men and women passed rather than be unfaithful to their ideals. On the 16th of January, 1664–65, there were ninety-nine Quakers in Newgate under sentence of transportation, one of whom was a shoemaker of Mile End, whose brief trial is recorded by Besse.[1] He had been taken at a meeting, and was asked by the justices where he dwelt. "I have a dwelling," he answered, "where neither thief, murderer, nor persecutor

[1] *Sufferings*, vol. i. p. 404.

can come"; and being asked again where that was, he replied, "In God." He was sent to Bridewell as a vagabond; and making at the sessions a like reply to the question of the judge as to where his dwelling-place was, he was sentenced to be transported with three malefactors to Virginia, and there to be sold as a slave for seven years. Before the close of the month ninety-six more Quakers were brought into Newgate from their meetings, and at the end of the year twenty-five Friends amongst the Newgate prisoners had died as a result of the treatment they had received and the insanitary overcrowding of the jail. Nor was it in London and the large towns only that this went on, for in the same year there were as many as twenty-nine persons sentenced to transportation from the little town of Hertford alone, eight of them for being present at a silent meeting.[1]

Yet this persecution doubtless served to purify the Society of unworthy elements, and the manner in which the Quakers bore their sufferings impressed even such an unsympathetic though not unkindly nature as that of Pepys, who records in his diary his feelings at seeing the poor folk led off to prison from their conventicles, going "like lambs, without

[1] Besse, *Sufferings*, vol. i. p. 248.

any resistance"! The effect upon stronger and deeper natures was different; for it was at this period that William Penn and Robert Barclay threw in their lot with **1667** Friends. The sudden change in Penn's case from favour at court to disownment by his father, the admiral, and a nine-months' imprisonment in the Tower, was test indeed of earnestness of conviction; nor was it altogether an easy task for a scholar like Barclay to follow his father's example in becoming one of a people hated as heretics and despised as ignorant and illiterate men. Both brought their natural gifts and previous training to the service of the Society they had joined, and both possessed powers of statesmanship which were of great value in building up its organisation. But though Barclay was able to set forth the principles of the Quakers in a way none had attempted before him, and to challenge the theological scholarship of Europe, and though Penn might have been expected to take a position of pre-eminence as the founder of a new colony and commonwealth, and author of a unique experiment in civic government, yet neither endeavoured to take any place of peculiar authority apart from their fellow-workers. They were simply Quaker preachers like the rest, and took their part gladly with men of modest intellectual powers and humble rank, as brothers of a common service.

They were following thus the example of one who under the previous Government had also been willing to sacrifice all prospects of material advantage by joining the Quakers, and who now bore his full share of persecution. This was Isaac Penington, the son of the Puritan Lord Mayor who bore so large a part in the struggle between king and Parliament. He had long been one of the Seekers, and had gone through much spiritual suffering before he joined the Quakers, to find with them a calm which no persecutions could destroy. Under the Restoration he was imprisoned six times, once for holding a meeting for worship in his own house, and another time for attending a Quaker's funeral at Amersham. Twice he was imprisoned in Aylesbury Jail during the pleasure of the Earl of Bridgewater, without any kind of trial, for more than two years in all, confined in damp rooms and exposed to the contagion of the plague. Finally, he was kept for a year and three-quarters in Reading Jail under sentence of præmunire, and was deprived of his Buckinghamshire estates. Yet in the midst of all, in spite of loss of health and property, he was

able to impress all who knew him by the
gentle charm of his nature, and to aid the
spread of Quaker views by his writings, which
still speak to us of the calm and joy of the
mystic reconciled with God and man.[1]

Amid all those who suffered for their faith
under Charles II. there is perhaps no figure
more attractive than that of the aged William
Dewsbury, one of Fox's earliest converts
and fellow-workers. He underwent imprisonments in Warwick lasting in all for nineteen
years, and of these four years were spent in
strict confinement in the common jail. In
the later years of his imprisonment he was
allowed to live at the sergeant's ward, and
here he was cheered by the presence of his
twelve-year-old grandchild Mary Sam, who
came from her parents' home in Bedfordshire
to live with him in the jail. At length, however, the child fell ill and died, and when the
old man was at last released by the proclamation of King James II., in 1686, he was so
enfeebled by his long imprisonment that he
tells us he was often compelled to rest twice
or thrice, for faintness, on his walk from his
home to the meeting in the town. But what

[1] Collected after his death in 1679 and published
under the title of *The Works of the Long Mournful and
Sorely Distressed Isaac Penington*, 2 pt., 1681, 4to.

illumines this record of suffering is the beautiful spirit in which the man bore all his hardships ; gentle and unrepining to the end, he bore no ill-will against his persecutors, and saw in the evils he suffered a means by which he hoped to win them to the truth. From time to time he would write letters to Friends throughout the country or in prison like himself, which bring back to one's memory the glowing faith of Ignatius of Antioch, but breathe a gentler and kindlier spirit than that of the old martyr bishop. When he was confined for the last time at Warwick (under the charge that he was a Jesuit in disguise) he wrote to exhort Friends to be ready with him "to forsake wife and children, to give up our lives daily in tumults, strifes, bloodshed, with cruel sufferings, both in prison and when at liberty, for to bring enemies out of enmity in the light to be in union with God." [1]

At the close of his life, in the spring of 1688, he came up to London, where he had useful service ; but before long he was seized with the recurrent fever which he had had for many years in prison, and he returned home by short journeys to die. On his death-bed he spoke to the Friends about

[1] *The Faithful Testimony of . . . William Dewsbury* [1689], 4to, p. 354.

him of the way in which the Divine power
had sustained him, since his first call as a
minister : " Therefore, Friends, be faithful,
and trust in the Lord your God ; for this I
can say, I never since played the coward, but
joyfully entered prisons as palaces, telling
mine enemies to hold me there as long as
they could. And in the prison-house I sang
praises to my God, and esteemed the bolts
and locks put upon me as jewels ; and in the
name of the eternal God I always got the
victory." [1]

The work done by George Fox amidst
this time of persecution was of great
importance, and it was during its stress
that he devoted himself to establishing the
Church organisation of the Quakers upon a
firm basis. After well nigh three years of
imprisonment, he had been released in 1666
from Scarborough, and for a time was able
to travel about more freely, suggesting in
1667 the starting of a school for Quaker
boys at Waltham, and one for girls at
Shacklewell, "for instructing them in what-
soever things were civil and useful in the
creation ; " [2] for the early Quakers were no

[1] Edward Smith, *The Life of William Dewsbury*.
1836, 8vo, p. 278.

[2] Journal, ii. p. 89.

enemies to knowledge, as such a life as
Thomas Ellwood's well shows. In 1669 he
1669   visited Ireland, and on his return
he simply chronicles one of the
great events of his life, his marriage to the
brave woman who had so long shared his
faith and already suffered for it. Margaret
Fell had been a widow for more than ten
years, and was now visiting a married
daughter in Bristol. Before the marriage
took place she called all her children, at the
request of Fox, that they and theirs might
agree that they suffered no loss by the marriage. Her six daughters gave it their hearty
approval ; her son alone, who had no sympathy with the Quakers and was a spendthrift
eager to get more money into his hands, had
no liking for the match.

George and Margaret Fox were each so
intent on their work and so united in the
whole object of their lives, that they were
willing for its sake to undergo long separa-
tions, and the first came speedily. Fox and
his wife parted not long after the wedding,
she returning to Swarthmore and he to his
work in the South. After about a month of
travelling service he wrote to her arranging
that they should meet again in Leicestershire, but in the meantime Margaret Fox

had been carried off on an order from the
Council to Lancaster Jail under a sentence of
præmunire, for which she had already been
imprisoned at intervals from the year 1663.
Fox endeavoured in vain to procure her
release, until 1671, when, on the eve of his
setting sail with a company of Quaker
ministers for the West Indies and America,
she was at length able to rejoin him. In the
interval had come the sharp outburst of persecution which followed the passing of the
Second Conventicle Act in 1670. Fox tells
us how he went at once when the Act had
come into force to the meeting at Gracechurch Street, where he expected that the
storm was most likely to begin.

1670   A guard had been set to prevent
any from entering the meeting-house; the
Quakers met in the courtyard. As George
Fox was speaking, an informer came up with
a constable and soldiers, and he was carried
away before the Lord Mayor. Unexpectedly
he was released, and at once returned to the
meeting. Thus throughout London and
over the whole country the Quakers continued to meet in spite of the Act. Their
meeting-houses were closed, or even pulled
down, but they gathered together in the
street outside or amid the ruins. In some

cases when the adult members of the meeting
were all in prison, their children met together
at the accustomed place of prayer. [1]

In August, 1670, came the famous trial of
William Penn and William Mead, for taking
part at a meeting for worship in Gracechurch
Street, ending at length in their acquittal,
though the Recorder sent jury and prisoners
to Newgate together in spite of the verdict.
For many months during this time of suffering Fox lay at death's door at Enfield. At
length he was able to resume his work, and
succeeded in obtaining his wife's freedom in
time for her to see him again before he started
for America. His work now lay more especially in confirming and strengthening the
groups of Quakers which were already
gathered together, and in establishing in all
parts a form of Church organisation ; and it
is characteristic of the later years of his life
that his Journal makes frequent reference to
that Divine principle in the soul for which he
bore constant witness, not merely as of old

---

[1] A striking instance of this occurred at Bristol,
when, throughout the summer of 1682, the meeting
was kept up by the children, though the boys were
punished by the stocks and by unmerciful flogging
(Besse, vol. i. p. 66). The children at Cambridge and
at Reading showed similar faith and courage.

as " the Light," but as " the Seed of God," or
simply " the Seed," " the Immortal Seed."

The metaphor seems to show how Fox
wished to express his consciousness that,
whether in the individual soul or in the
community, the Divine immanence involves
a process of living and organic growth.
Amid the stress of persecution he grew in-
creasingly sensible of the interdependence of
one life upon another, and the importance
of a system of religious fellowship which
would express this relationship. As one
turns the later pages of his Journal one is
struck with his deep enthusiasm for this
work of organisation and his faith that it
was the expression of an eternal truth. He
rejoices again and again that " the Gospel
order " is set up, and is confident that this
will endure when other forms of Church
government have passed away. However
little it may seem to some that the Society
of Friends has actually realised the thought
of Fox, it may still be possible to recognise
in this conception of an organisation in which
the aristocratic and democratic ideals are
united in the higher ideal of theocracy, the
pattern of Church government which shall
endure when less perfect forms have dis-
appeared, or have been raised to its level.

It was after his return from America in
1673 that George Fox suffered imprisonment
for the last time.   He was journeying north-
ward with his wife, when a meeting in a barn
which they attended was made the ground
for his arrest and imprisonment in Worcester
Jail, along with his wife's son-in-law, Thomas
Lower.   At the time of his arrest, Fox had
been hoping to proceed to Leicestershire to
be present at his aged mother's death-bed,[1] at
her earnest desire, but he was not now to see
her again.   Twice he was sent up to London
to the King's Bench, and at length, after prolonged delay, at the close of the year 1674,
he was finally set free by proclamation of the
court.

Henceforth he was to share his Friends'
sufferings only in spirit, but though, after two
or three years of rest at Swarthmore, he was
strong enough to make two journeys to Hol-
land, one extended into Northern Germany,
he never regained the health and strength
which he had lost through repeated imprisonments, and during the last years of his life

[1] It is characteristic of his reticence as to all personal matters that we learn this almost by accident
from his Journal, through the letter of protest addressed by the prisoners to the Lord-Lieutenant
inserted in it (Journal, vol. ii. p. 207).

travelled but little away from London. His
duty kept him there rather than in the comfortable home at Swarthmore, and in spite of
bodily weakness he was active up to the end,
visiting the sick, attending meetings, and
corresponding with Friends at home and
abroad. He was able to witness the release
of 1,460 Quaker prisoners by James II., and
to see the Declaration of Indulgence legalised
by the Act of Toleration.

Margaret Fox felt that she could not leave
her work in the North, but she made more
than one long journey that she might be
with her husband, the last one when she was
seventy-six years of age, about half a year
before his death, a visit which she tells us
was the most full of comfort of all the times
she was in London.

When at length the end came, George Fox
was ready. Three days before his death he
preached with great power and
1690   solemnity at Gracechurch Street
meeting. We do not know what his message
then was, but the words which he spoke to
some who came to see him on his death-bed
seem fittingly to close not only his own brave
life, but the era of persecution the end of
which he had witnessed: "All is well; the Seed
of God reigns over all, and over death itself."

VII

ORGANISATION

THE student of Church history will note
with interest how not a few of the
problems that confront him in the wider
story of the Church are reproduced in that
of the small body of the Society of Friends.
The three orders to which one school attaches
so much importance—deacons, presbyters, and
bishops—are preserved curiously enough in
the Quaker names of ministers, elders, and
overseers. And just as, in recent years, the
keenest controversy and the most painstaking
research of Church historians have been connected with the original meaning and nature
of the offices of presbyter and bishop, so too
we shall find that students of Quaker history
are met with a like problem. At the close
of the eighteenth century it was questioned
whether "elders" and "overseers" were inter-
changeable names, while at a later date

Robert Barclay, of Tottenham, maintained the view that in the seventeenth century "elders" were nothing more nor less than "acknowledged ministers."

During the first few years of the Quaker movement there existed no sort of organisation amongst the "Children of Light," as they were called. Indeed, George Fox had no idea of founding a separate religious body; he simply went about proclaiming his message to all, and trusting that the truth he preached would set men free, wherever the message was heeded. They, in their turn, would become messengers of the Evangel, and so it might be hoped that in no short time the whole body of professing Christians would come to realise their helplessness without this personal religion, and would rule their lives and worship by faith in the immediate presence of the Light of Christ in the soul of each. George Fox had probably no more idea of founding a new sect than had Luther of separating Christendom into two great divisions of Protestant and Catholic. Their object was to set forth anew the living Gospel, to draw men to it and away from shams, to proclaim a great and universal message, not to organise a party or create a new association of people.

So for the first few years, as Fox and the early Quaker preachers moved about over the country, the word "Friends" meant simply all who were friendly to the truth they proclaimed and lived in harmony with it. All over the land they had found little groups of "Seekers" who had already anticipated one side of the teaching of Fox as to the failure and unreality of a formal Christianity, which lacked the spirit and power of Christ. These Seekers had now become Friends; they had been accustomed often already to meet together in silence, under a sense of common need and dependence upon the Unseen, and thus the nucleus of regular meetings for worship already existed in many places.

As persecution speedily followed the new wave of religious life, and all the prejudices of the local magistrates were brought into play against the Quakers, it was a perfectly natural outcome of the friendly relationship which had grown up between the Friends of the new movement that, as one and another suffered imprisonment, those that remained free would take care for them and provide, when needful, for their families. As the persecution increased, and it appeared clear that it would be of no short duration, it became reasonable that these efforts to help the suffering should be put on a more certain basis, and hence it was found desirable for one group of Friends to join with others who might be in greater need, or perhaps in some cases freer to help. Thus arose the first beginnings of Church organisation amongst the Quakers, as a simple act of mutual protection and helpfulness amongst men who shared the same ideals and were suffering for the same cause.

The first "Monthly Meeting" appears to have been that of the Friends of Durham, **1653** which was started in 1653. It was then arranged that "some of every meeting" should come together "every first Seventh Day of each month," principally to make arrangements with regard to Friends in prison, or in need of other help, such as widows and orphans or the families of prisoners. Shortly afterwards a Monthly Meeting was started at Swarthmore, no doubt on similar lines. During this year George Fox was often at Swarthmore and in the neighbourhood, and also passed through Durham holding meetings, but he does not make any mention, in his Journal at this point, of the setting up of Monthly Meetings, which may perhaps have

11

occurred while he was in Carlisle Jail. When, **1654** in 1654, however, he turns southward again, he says he did so "when the Churches were settled in the north," which would seem to imply the formation of definite congregations of Friends.

But though this organisation existed at so early a date in the northern centre of Quakerism, it was only much later that it became generally adopted, and that at the cost of great efforts and in face of a controversy whose bitterness may well puzzle us to-day.

In the meantime, throughout a greater part of the country, the only link connecting the different congregations of Friends was formed by the travelling preachers going from meeting to meeting. At an early date, however, we find frequent allusions in George Fox's Journal to "General Meetings." These would seem to have been, originally, simply meetings attended by a large number of people from some distance round, not exclusively Friends. [1]

This was certainly the case at the first General Meeting of which we have knowledge, that at Swannington, in 1654. "Travel-

[1] Journal, vol. ii. p. 12.

ling through Derbyshire," says George Fox,
1654 "I visited Friends till I came
to Swannington, in Leicestershire,
where there was a general meeting, to which
many Ranters, Baptists, and other professors
came; for great contests there had been with
them, and with the priests of that town. To
this meeting several friends came from various
parts, as John Audland, Francis Howgill, and
Edward Pyot from Bristol, and Edward Burrough from London; and several were convinced in those parts. The Ranters made a
disturbance and were very rude; but at last
the Lord's power came over them and they
were confounded. . . ."[1]

At such meetings it was natural that collections should be made for the poor, and
to pay the travelling expenses of "public
friends" who needed this help, and inquiries
were made as to the suffering of Friends in
different parts of the country, and advice
given by many who had been Justices themselves, as to means of redress. Thus we
have at once the germs of a "business meeting" for Church affairs, and it would seem
that minutes made at the General Meeting
were taken home by Friends attending it in
their own districts.

[1] Journal, i. 199.

These General Meetings seem to have been at times especially for the Friends of one county.[1] At other times the General Meetings were wider in scope. Thus in his Journal for 1660 George Fox writes : " And so to Skipton, where there was a General Meeting of men Friends out of many counties, concerning the affairs of the Church. . . . To this Meeting came Friends out of most parts of the nation, for it was about business relating to the Church both in this nation and beyond the seas. Several years before, when I was in the North I was moved to recommend the setting up of this Meeting for that service : for many Friends suffered in divers parts of the nation, their goods were taken from them contrary to the law and they understood not how to help them-

[1] Thus in 1663 George Fox notes : "From the meeting near Collumpton we went to Taunton, where we had a large meeting. Then next day we came to a General Meeting in Somersetshire, which was very large," and a little later . . . "we came to Street, and to William Beeton's at Puddimore, where we had a very large General Meeting." Similarly when in Cornwall a little earlier he speaks of going to Loveday Hambley's, "where we had a General Meeting for the whole county, and all was quiet." In 1668 they held a "General Meeting for all the country" at the same house.

selves, or where to seek redress. But after this Meeting was set up, several Friends who had been magistrates, and others that understood something of the law came thither, and were able to inform Friends, and to assist them in gathering up the sufferings, that they might be laid before the justices, judges, or Parliament. This Meeting had stood several years and divers justices and captains had come to break it up; but when they understood the business Friends met about, and saw their books and accounts of collections for relief of the poor, how we took care one county to help another, and to help our friends beyond the seas, and provide for our poor, that none of them should be chargeable to their parishes, &c., the justices and officers confessed we did their work, and passed away peaceably and lovingly, commending Friends' practice. Sometimes there would come two hundred of the poor of other people, and would wait there till the Meeting was done (for all the country knew we met about the poor,) and after the Meeting Friends would send to the bakers for bread, and give everyone of those poor people a loaf, how many soever there were of them; for we were taught to 'do good unto all; though especially to the household of faith.' After this Meet-

ing I visited Friends in their Meetings, till
I came to Lancaster, whence I went to
Robert Widder's, and so to Arnside, where
I had a General Meeting for all the
Friends in Westmorland, Cumberland, and
Lancashire." [1]

Thus it is clear that these General Meetings
contained the germ both of the present
Quarterly Meetings and of the
central Yearly Meeting. The
latter name seems first to occur in the case
of the Yearly Meeting at Scalehouse, near
Skipton, in 1658, which sent out an epistle
recommending a collection in aid of the
religious visits of Friends "beyond the
seas."

1658

In the same year George Fox's Journal
gives an account of another Yearly Meeting
in Bedfordshire, that at Scalehouse having
been more especially for the North Country.
"After some time we came to John Crook's
house, where a General Yearly Meeting for
the whole nation was appointed to be held.
This Meeting lasted three days, and many
Friends from most parts of the nation came
to it; so that the inns and towns around
were filled, for many thousands of people
were at it." [2]

[1] Journal, i. 469.   [2] Ibid., i. 418.

The Minutes of this Meeting contain what is perhaps the earliest reference to " Overseers " in the new Society. " That collections be timely made for the poor that are so indeed, as they are moved, according to order, for relief of prisoners, and for other necessary uses, as need shall require ; and all moneys so collected on account thereof to be taken from which any need may be supplied, as made known by the Overseers in every Meeting ; that no private ends may be answered, but all brought to the light, that the Gospel be not slandered.

" That care be taken for the families and goods of such as are called forth unto the Ministry, or are imprisoned for truth's sake ; that no creature be lost for want of the creatures."

There seems already to have been some fear lest the last injunction should be misunderstood, for at the Durham General Meeting in 1659 a Minute was made " That all collections made by Friends at their Monthly Meetings as also at their General Meetings be for the needs of the Churches in general, and not be limited for those that are in the Ministry ; who will be as much grieved as others offended to have a maintenance or hire raised on purpose for them."

The Quaker organisation was evidently developing, but it was still without any unifying scheme of Church government, though it is clear that in London there did exist some definite arrangements for the care of the prisoners for some time before the Monthly Meetings were set up. As Thos. Ellwood tells us in his Journal, in 1662, " an excellent order, even in those early days, was practised among the Friends of that City (London), by which there were certain Friends of either sex appointed to have the oversight of the prisons in every Quarter, and to take care of all Friends, the poor especially, that should be committed thither."

But as these measures of orderly arrangement increased, opposition to them became more and more marked. The first difficulties arose curiously enough in what seems now an extraordinary controversy, as to whether or no Friends should remove their hats during vocal prayer.

George Fox had always given as one of his reasons for refusing this honour to men, that it was one peculiarly due to God, and he insisted on the duty of keeping to this instinctive mark of reverence in approaching the Divine Presence. **1661** John Perrot, who was the leader of the new party, wrote from the Madhouse at Rome (where the not unkindly Inquisitors had imprisoned him) to protest against this formality. He was willing, however, to allow those who felt so drawn to throw themselves on their faces and loose their shoes from off their feet during prayer, as for this he was able to find Scripture precedent.[1] In spite of his eccentricity, Perrot managed to draw a number of Friends after him, and these published their view in 1673 in a book entitled *The Spirit of the Hat*, protesting against all artificial forms in worship.

1673

In the meantime Fox must have realised the results which would follow if the wild individualism of Perrot's friends should have its way, and he met the crisis by going through the country, setting up Monthly Meetings for discipline in districts which did not already possess them. It has been suggested by Dr. Thos. Hodgkin[2] that it was during his long imprisonment at Scarborough Castle in 1665

---

[1] " He not only," says Sewel, " insisted on retaining his hat in the Meeting while prayer was being made, but made another extravagant step and let his beard grow."

[2] *George Fox*, 1896, 8vo., p. 205, *seq.*

that the necessity of this work came home to
him. He knew that Friends were suffering,
perhaps more severely than ever before ; he
had still present with him the need of a
thorough organisation for self-defence, both
against persecutions from without and
dangers from within. He had not forgotten
the trouble that had come in the past to his
friends through the fall of James Nayler :
John Perrot and other strange spirits were
still active and might at any time cause like
difficulties ; there was need for the new body
to have power to exclude from its fellowship
such as were doing harm to the cause of
truth.

George Fox simply mentions the first
occasion on which this concern
1666 bore fruit, in his Journal for the
year 1666. " Then I was moved of the
Lord to recommend the setting up of five
Monthly Meetings of men and women in
the city of London (besides the Women's
Meetings and the Quarterly Meetings) to
take care of God's glory, and to admonish
and exhort such as walked disorderly or
carelessly, and not according to truth. For
whereas Friends had had only Quarterly
Meetings, now the truth was spread, I was
moved to recommend the setting up of

Monthly Meetings throughout the nation.
And the Lord showed me what I must do,
and how the men's and women's Monthly and
Quarterly Meetings should be ordered and
established in this and other nations; and
that I should write to those where I did not
come, to do the same." [1]

From this time forth the organisation of
the Society became Fox's great concern, and
his travels both in England and America
were largely concerned with it. With great
insight he perceived the dangers of a congregational system which would isolate weak
Meetings from strong ones and give undue
power to local influences: he felt that the
grouping of neighbouring Meetings into
Monthly Meetings, as already practised in
the North, should be carried out throughout
the country, and that these should be further
co-ordinated by Quarterly Meetings for
larger districts and a Yearly Meeting to
unite the whole country. Feeling as he did
the importance of the place of women in the
Church, he also saw that there should be
Monthly Meetings for women as well as men,
the women's Meetings taking especial care
for the sick and poor.

During the Commonwealth provision had

[1] Vol. ii. p. 80.

been made for civil marriage before a magistrate in addition to the religious ceremony in Church, but now the former practice was given up, and the clergy attacked Friends' marriages as invalid. George Fox saw the need of guarding against occasions of stumbling in this matter, and the careful regulation of marriages was one of the chief objects for which he urged the establishment of the Monthly Meetings.

But all this caused great offence to many Friends who had been attracted to the new Society by the individualistic side of the teaching of its early preachers : the Light which lighteth every man was, they said, sufficient guide to each. For a group of Meetings to order individual Meetings to take action in things for which they might have no concern was to override true Christian liberty : still less then had any Church organisation, they said, right to judge individual members or settle disputes between them (this being a duty Fox laid strongly upon the Monthly Meetings). They even questioned the right to exclude individuals from membership on moral or doctrinal grounds, since what the Meeting regarded as sin and error might not appear as such to the individual in question, according to the Light that was given him, which alone could be his standard of life and conduct.

Several prominent ministers now definitely took the side of these individualists, the two leaders being John Wilkinson and John Story, of Preston, in Westmorland. They were joined by Thos. Curtis, of Reading, and Wm. Rogers, a wealthy Bristol merchant, with several other well-known men. Their bitterest opposition seems to have been to the setting up of women's Meetings, which they considered a " monstrous " and unheard-of innovation. They opposed any disciplinary action being taken against Friends who went to be married by a clergyman, or those who paid tithes, and were only willing to allow of the use of Monthly and General Meetings in so far as they were informal gatherings attended by those who felt free so to do, their recommendations being only followed where individual meetings could unite with the proposals. They also recommended Friends to meet in secret, in order to avoid persecution, and were in favour of the closing of Meeting-houses, where needful or expedient. They disliked the provision of money to assist travelling ministers in their journeys abroad, and evidently sympathised with the Quietist ideal of worship, for

we find the complaint made against them
that they objected to a congregation giving
outward utterance to its feelings, and tried to
suppress " groanings, sighings, soundings, and
singings," congregational singing being at
the time not altogether unknown amongst
Friends, as is seen by the hymn written by
Catherine Evans, the music of which is
printed by Sewel in his Dutch edition.

Apart from these deep-lying questions of
principle, opposition to the personal influence
of George Fox undoubtedly had much to do
with the movement. This magnetic power
over men, to which so many passages in his
Journal bear witness, sometimes acted as a
repelling force; and the new discipline was
represented by the seceders as an attempt to
set up a hierarchic system, with Fox as head
and Pope controlling all. Great efforts were
made to check any separation, and for some
time the schism was avoided.[1]

[1] In 1673 an epistle was sent out to be read in
Quarterly Meetings, Monthly Meetings, and other
Meetings, signed by a number of weighty Friends,
including Wm. Penn, Robert Barclay, George
Whitehead, Stephen Crisp, Alexander Parker, John
Raunce, and William Rogers (who both afterwards
joined the separation), dealing with the need for
kindly wisdom in the exercise of Church discipline ;
"elders and overseers" "must not be self-willed"

In 1676 a conference was held at Drawell, near Sedbergh, at which Story and Wilkinson **1676** signed a paper of recantation; but the controversy was not stopped. These two Friends, with their followers, seceded from the main body of their own

nor "soon angry." The epistle pleads " that none join to such a singular spirit as would lead him to be sole judge in his own case, but in the restoring and healing spirit of Christ both the offended and the offender may for the truth's sake submit to the power of God in His own people, in those cities, places or counties with such Friends as they with the parties concerned shall call to their assistance; for they do and will judge for God: and if any will not give up his matter to the judgment of truth in his people, he doth but render himself and his cause suspicious, and that he wants the sense of the fellow-ship of the Body: and as Friends keep in Wisdom and patience concerning such it will come over him and be his Burden. . . . And though a general care be not laid upon every member touching the good order and government in the Churche's affairs, nor have many travelled therein, yet the Lord hath laid it more upon some in whom He hath opened Council for that end (and particularly in our dear Brother and God's faithful labourer, G. F.) for the help of many and God hath in His wisdom afforded those helps and Governments in the Churches which are not to be despised, being in subjection to Christ the one head and Lawgiver, answering His witness in all" (Devonshire House MSS.).

Meeting, and then went up and down the
country inducing others to do the like. In
Reading, Bristol,[1] Chippenham, Alston, and
elsewhere, the seceders being trustees of the
Meeting-houses, took possession, and kept
Friends from using them for some years.
There was a large number of Friends in
Wiltshire who sided with the secession, and
after the death of John Story they published
a glowing testimony to his character and life-
work, which was answered by Thos. Camm, a
native of Story's own meeting, who told his
admirers how their apostle got Friends there
to meet in secluded gills and corners of the
hills, with a lad on the watch to give a token
to him if any sign of the soldiers should
appear, he having told Friends that if they
would but press his foot he would instantly
stop preaching; or how on another occasion
he bade Friends keep the doors barred against
the soldiers while he himself hid in a cock-
loft, leaving the Meeting to fend for itself.

This may not seem a very worthy attack
upon Story, and at first sight it may appear
that the seceders' refusal to disown members
for marriage before a clergyman or the payment of tithes showed a greater liberality and
width of spirit than that of the main section
of Quakers. But we hardly realise in judging

[1] In Bristol W. Rogers, who became a trustee of the Meeting-house
in 1680, got possession of the title deeds, and when the city authorities
seized the house would lend no help in maintaining the Meeting's claim.

thus what this attitude meant in such a time
of terrible stress. The second Conventicle
Act of Charles II. had been passed, and
persecution was at its height. The Quakers
almost alone amongst Dissenters stood up
openly for religious liberty by continuing to
meet in public, despite the law, in their old
Meeting-houses, or on the sites of them when
they had been pulled down. To avoid persecution by meeting in private, to encourage
compromise and time-serving in the matter
of weddings and tithe-paying was in effect
to give up the struggle, or to retire from it
defeated. Only by presenting a united front,
and acting together as one body, were Friends
able to persevere and win the victory they
ultimately did. The separatists aimed at a
liberty of conscience which meant anarchy in
the Church. They were only willing for a
Minute of disapproval on account of some
moral offence to be recorded when the offend-
ing party himself was willing for this to be
done, and it is obvious that this would mean
that the most serious cases could not be dealt
with at all by Church discipline.

For a short time George Whitehead was
inclined to be drawn aside by the separatists'
views, and Thos. Ellwood had at an earlier
date been one of John Perrot's "hatmen," but

he had soon seen his mistake, and now entered the lists on behalf of Fox. Wm. Rogers, of **1680** Bristol, in 1680, wrote a lengthy work entitled *The Christian Quaker Distinguished from the Apostate and Innovator*, in which he made a bitter attack on George Fox, to which Ellwood in 1682 replied. Rogers returned to the fight in a pamphlet in doggerel verse, to which Ellwood again rejoined in like form in his *Rogeromastix* in 1685. Rogers contrasted the new ordered liberty of Church Government which Fox pleaded for with the old individual freedom of the early days :—

"The Gospel loud did cry : our Law's the light,
Liberty of conscience is men's right ;
But when that Fox about Church Government
More than the Gospel time and labour spent
I' the stead of liberty of conscience he
Said Liberty of th' Gospel, it must be.

When he had fram'd i' th' Church a Government,
Preachers, approved by Man, beyond seas went,
Who when they wanted moneys to proceed
The Church Her cash then did supply their need
If they their motion freely did submit
To the London Church, and do as She thought
    fit."

He went on to describe the growing power

and importunity of the London Church and
"Morning Meeting" of ministers and elders,
held weekly in London :—

"At length her papers, like to briefs did cry
   For money, money for the Ministry."

The worthy merchant had occasionally to
help out his limping verse with such tags of
prose as "to procede," "hence I conclude,"
over which Ellwood makes merry : he too
will write verse for verse, he says :—

"If verse without offense that may be call'd
   Which is delivered in rhimes so bald,
   So flat, so dull, so rough, so void of grace,
   Where sympathy and cadence have no place
   So full of chasmes, stuck with prosy pegs
   Whereon his tir'd muse might rest her legs
   (Not having wings) and take new breath that then
   She might, with much adoe, hop on again."

Point for point he answers Rogers, maintaining that Fox did not send preachers about
from place to place at his own mere will, but
only with the joint concern of those who went,
just as Paul might lay it upon Timothy and
Epaphroditus to take up some special work ;
and he repels the attack on the payment of
travelling expenses of ministers bravely :—

"May none beyond seas go, but who can spare
   Sufficient of their own the charge to bear ?

Must Christ be so confin'd He may not send
Any but such as have estates to spend?
God bless us from such doctrine and such
    teachers
As will admit of none but wealthy preachers."

Probably the ablest contribution to the discussion of the problem was that given in 1676 by Robert Barclay in *The Anarchy of the Ranters*.

1676

Barclay distinguishes between the true Church order and discipline and the hierarchic system with which it was confused by the separatists. Business meetings should be concerned with widows, orphans, and education, the settling of disputes between Friends, marriages, and questions of discipline in delinquencies ; these might be considered as " outward things," while from the inward side the Church meetings should guard against the danger of erroneous teaching.

Barclay holds up against the separatists' view of individual liberty under the guidance of the Spirit, the higher truth of the subordination of the members to the fulfilment each of their own office in the body. The Spirit was not merely a guide to the individual, but to the Church, and in every true Church assembly the infallible Spirit must be present, though of course no mere numerical majority could be any judge of His will. It was some years before the controversy was settled, but finally, as Sewel says,[1] the separatists melted like snow, a number eventually admitting their error and returning to the main body of Friends. The result was indeed an inevitable one, for no society of men could endure for long whose principles were so antagonistic to all common responsibility and all hope of organic growth, which necessarily involves the subordination of the individual to the wider life of the whole body.

Robert Barclay, of Tottenham, in his *Inner Life of the Religious Societies of the Commonwealth*, has maintained the view that the influence of this separation was far deeper than is usually supposed, and that it ultimately resulted in a gradual victory for the Quietist party after the death of Fox and his contemporaries. This he connects with the slow growth in power of "lay elders," his view being that in the early days of the Quaker movement the elders were exclusively ministers. One cannot help sharing the opinion of Dr. Charles Evans, of Philadelphia, that Barclay's view on this point is unconsciously prejudiced by his enthusiasm for the Methodist system of

Sewel, vol. ii. p. 437.

preachers established by John Wesley. Men like Thomas Ellwood, even in the early days of the Society of Friends, were greatly valued as elders and for their help in carrying out the organisation of the Church, although they were not public ministers. All the evidence that we have, however, seems to show that such Friends were quite exceptional. It was not till almost the middle of the eighteenth century that the elders were largely men and women who seldom or never themselves took part in the ministry.

Before passing from the question of the growth of the early Quaker Society, it may be worth while to picture for a moment the condition of things in the later years of the seventeenth century, when the new polity was already in good working order. A large amount of material for this study is in existence amongst the MSS. at Devonshire House, Bishopsgate Street, and amongst the documents of the various Monthly and Quarterly Meetings in the provinces.[1]

Taking as an instance Settle Monthly

[1] A most interesting study of the life of country meetings in the Southern counties will be found in the work of Thos. William Marsh, *Some Records of the Early Friends in Surrey and Sussex*. London, 1886, 4to.

Meeting, whose documents are now preserved
at Leeds, we find in 1666 this little group of
five or six country congregations collecting
the sum of £12 19s. 3d. "for the use of
Friends who suffered loss by fire at London."
At the same time there is a collection of
£7 13s. 4d. "for the supply of Friends in
prison and for the service of the truth in
generall." The latter entry represents a
constantly recurring feature in the early
Minutes : such collections were independent
of those for the poor of the district itself,
which were made with great regularity. In
connection with the care of the poor we shall
find such entries as that referring to the
payment of fees for a poor apprentice.

The Meeting also records with care the
arrival of Friends' books (which came from
London through the Quarterly Meeting at
York), and arranges for their circulation
amongst the various Meetings. There are
frequent entries, such as that of 6 xii. 1694 :
" The collection of books of Robert Barclay
and William Dewsbury is this day gone into
Bolland and to stay two months."

Arrangements were also made for the
interchange of visits between different congregations, as is seen in such an entry as that
of 7 i. 169¾ : " It is agreed this day that

Rilston Meeting Friends or Friend do attend Starrhouse Meeting this first month, Salterforth Meeting 2nd Month, Settle Meeting the 3rd month, Bentham Meeting the 4th month, and Bolland Meeting the fifth month, and then Rilston to begin again, but if any of the said Meeting do find they cannot attend the said Meetings as herein set downe, the one to acquaint the monthly Meeting . . . so that some other Friend might supply their place."

Other entries of interest show that in 1682 two Friends were appointed in each Meeting as visitors to prevent and remove causes of stumbling through ill living, an office later known as that of overseer. (And cf. 2 vi. 1693.)

From time to time the Meeting has to disown some member for disorderly living, and the approval of proposals of marriage between different members, after due intervals for inquiry, is a constantly recurring subject. Occasionally too the Meeting disowns a member who has been married by a priest. As time goes on there is evidence of an increasing amount of centralisation. Thus, in 2 vii. 1696, "a general collection for the Yearly Meeting" of £2 14s. 2d. is sent up to the Quarterly Meeting at York, in direct

response to a request from the central
authority, while in 1692 (30 vi.) Samuel
Watson and William Ellis are appointed by
the Monthly Meeting to inquire the advice of
London Friends concerning a Friend "that
desires to take his first couzen's daughter to
wife." The Friends consulted were the
"Morning Meeting" of ministers and elders
which met weekly in London, and acted in
the early days of the Society in many ways
as an executive committee of the Yearly
Meeting.[1]

There does not appear to be evidence of
any custom of formal application for membership amongst the early Quakers; for the first
two generations of the Society persecution
was so severe that there was little to induce
men to join from unworthy motives, and those
who endeavoured to count as Quakers merely
with a view to receiving a share in the collec-

[1] The Minutes of the Morning Meeting for 22 vi.
1692 show that George Whitehead, John Field, and
Theodore Eccleston were appointed to draw up an
answer. A copy of this (signed by the two latter) is
preserved in William Ellis's collection of letters and
papers among the Settle MSS. at Leeds. The reply
refers to the Minute of the Yearly Meeting of 1675
against the marriage of first cousins, but cautiously
leaves the final decision in this case to the Monthly
Meeting.

tions for the poor and distressed would be soon detected. But even in the dark days of Charles II. the country districts had their times of quiet and peace, to which these old records bear witness. The following consecutive entries are typical of many more : " Settle Monthly Meeting holden the 6th day of the 7 mo. (85) when Friends having met together in the fear of the Lord having little outward concern to consider upon, being retired in their minds were refreshed together in the unity of the Spirit according to measure. Settle Monthly Meeting holden the 6th of the 8th month (85) Friends being met together in the fear of the Lord, where after consideration finding little outward business to be concern'd about, were refreshed in the feeling of the love of God to be shed abroad amongst them."

But it must not be supposed that the Friends of this remote district of Craven rested content with their times of quiet, mystical communion. From this little group of country Meetings two ministers, at least, went forth to wider service throughout the country, Samuel Watson journeying twice to Scotland, and William Ellis visiting both Ireland and Pennsylvania " in the service of truth " ; in their turn, these little Meetings received visits from well-known Quaker preachers from other parts of the country, and this interchange of service was only what went on throughout all the places where Meetings of Friends were held. Such visits were fruitful in the formation of lasting friendships, and the collection of papers formed by William Ellis preserves copies of a large number of letters which passed between him and Friends whom he had visited in America, or such fellow-ministers as William Edmondson. It was on the self-sacrifice of such men as these, who gave their whole lives freely to this service, that the Society of Friends as an organisation was built up, and the triumphant optimism with which they persevered against all discouragement cannot fail to strike all who read the story of their lives. " Therefore have I laboured," William Ellis tells us, " with my soul, body and substance that God hath given me, to bring truth up into dominion over all the country where I live, and to bring things to rights in our Particular and Monthly Meetings. . . . For though truth hath been preached and many convinced, yet for want of a fervent mind and faithfulness it might have been said as the prophet spoke concerning the people of old : ' Jacob is low, by whom shall he arise?' So that here hath been great need of faithful labourers that the sweetness and marrow of the Gospel may be brought up to peoples' understandings." Yet in spite of this he is able to say : " I am in great hopes great part of our valley will be convinced." [1]

The little Meeting-house at Airton, near Malham, which the good man laboured to build is still standing, and four or five Friends worship there to-day. But the change which two centuries have witnessed amongst the Society of Friends would hardly have come, had it not been for the loss of that combination of missionary vigour, careful organisation, and unselfish labour with the deep spiritual power to which that background of silent prayer and communion bears witness, and which all alike characterise the life of seventeenth-century Quakerism.

It was in the Monthly Meetings that the life of the early Quaker organisation was **1672** centred, but four times a year delegates from a group of these met along with others who were able to attend in the Quarterly Meeting, whose boundaries usually followed those of the different counties, while from 1672 onwards

[1] Ellis MS., p. 19. Among the Settle M.M. papers at Leeds.

these were in their turn grouped together
into a Yearly Meeting for the whole country,
which was regularly held from this date
onwards in London about Whitsuntide. The
earlier General Meetings which had preceded
this still continued to be held at Bristol and
in other places for long after this date,
though they soon ceased to have legislative
power. A Yearly Meeting for Women Friends
was held during the latter part of the
seventeenth and the first few years of the
eighteenth century in York, issuing an
Epistle and corresponding with subordinate
Meetings.

At length, after a considerable interval of
time, a Women's Yearly Meeting was established in 1784, in London, at the same time
as the Yearly Meeting for men, and since
1896 these have met in joint session when
matters involving decisions of importance to
the whole Society are under discussion.

It was early evident that the organisation
of the new Society would be incomplete
unless there were some body to which
recourse could be had in the intervals
between the annual General Meetings. This
seems to have been found at first in the
"Second Day Morning Meeting"—a gathering
of "public Friends," the leading ministers

who might be in London at the time, held every week at the house of one of their number. The Meeting probably began in an informal way, the Friends in question meeting at breakfast to talk over their work, and arrange which Meetings they should visit (almost always in groups of two) on the following Sunday. The first Minute of this Meeting preserved in its books dates from 15th vii. mo. 1673, and is simply headed, "At a meeting at G. Roberts'." It was then decided that "two of a sort of all books written by Friends be procured and kept together," along with one of all written against Friends, care being taken to see that suitable answers to these should be issued. It was also minuted "that one or two of those Friends who are appointed to take care of the press be desired to attend this Meeting every Second Day." This refers to a delegacy appointed by the Yearly Meeting in 1672, to have charge of the printing of Friends' books, which was done (at some risk at the hands of the authorities) by one or two Quaker printers, the various Quarterly Meetings each agreeing to take a certain number of the books printed, which were distributed by the delegates to duly appointed correspondents in each district. The " Morning Meeting" from this time takes care that all books thus printed are either read in full at its sittings or by a sub-committee, before they are sent to the press, and its subsequent Minutes deal very largely with this subject, pamphlets, letters, and books being frequently withheld for a while from publication, abridged, and corrected, or merely sent out in manuscript to the Meetings or parties concerned, and from time to time it is decided that some work is altogether unsuited for publication ;[1]

[1] A pleasant instance of the kindly way in which an author might be dealt with is seen in the following letter addressed to Judith Boultby, signed by Stephen Crisp and seven other Friends :—

"LONDON, *the* 18 4 *mo.* 1690.

"DEAR JUDITH,—Our love in the blessed truth salutes thee. This is to let thee know that we have read the paper thou left with us to be viewed and printed if we thought meet. Now as to that 'To the Women uncircumcised in heart' we think it not dependent with itself, for such as paint, adorn and dress like Jezebel are far from making clean the outside, and as to that to the magistrates we judge it not a fit time to print such account in this time of peace and quietness. But as to the 3rd, to the followers of the Lamb, we have made some little alterations in it as thou wilt see, which if thou sees meet thou mayest give forth coppies of it, it being short. Soe in the love of God we rest thy friends and brethren in the truth."

occasionally the final decision is left to the author himself, if he still feels the need to issue his message.

At its first recorded sitting the " Morning Meeting " directed Ellis Hookes, the clerk to the Yearly Meeting, to attend in future to record its Minutes, and after meeting for some time at various houses (such as that of Gerard Roberts, and that of Ann Travers, at Horslydown) it soon came to meet regularly in the clerk's chamber. We find this body approving the establishment of new Meetings in London or the neighbourhood, sending out (27 xi. 1689) a paper to the various Quarterly Meetings and Monthly Meetings on the question of marriages, answering epistles from abroad, and from various Quarterly Meetings at home, and receiving complaints as to Friends travelling as ministers whose services were felt to be misplaced,[1] and

---

[1] Thus in v. mo., 1689, Isaac Sadler, of Chelmsford, writes to the Morning Meeting, "signifying Friends' great grief and trouble concerning Mary Knight, rambling up and downe in Suffolk and Norfolk." Her husband was asked to use his influence with her, and two Friends "desired to speak at the Monthly Meeting at the Peel [in Clerkenwell] that they may give forth a testimony against her." The final disciplinary action was thus left to the judgment of the Monthly Meeting.

authorising others to go on service both at home and abroad.

Such exercise of authority by the Morning Meeting was strongly opposed by the individualistic section of the Society which Story and Wilkinson induced to separate from the main body of Friends. But the advantage of such a central authority was generally felt, and it was increased by the letter which George Fox left at his death requesting the Friends who had been accustomed from all parts of the world to write to him both to report persecutions and to ask advice, to write instead henceforth to the Morning Meeting.[1]

Gradually, however, this duty, along with others of importance, passed into the hands of a Meeting constituted upon a wider basis, in which, in 1901, the Morning Meeting itself was finally merged. This new Meeting, which came in time to act as the executive committee of the Society of Friends, was known as the Meeting for Sufferings.

The Yearly Meeting of 1675 had decided,

---

[1] The letter is minuted on xi. mo. 19th, 1690/91. "All Friends in all the world that used to write to me of all manner of things and passages [sufferings] and I did answer them, let them all write to the 2nd dayes meeting in London."

in view of the severe persecution which
1675   Friends were then undergoing, to
call a conference of representatives
from all the Quarterly Meetings to consult as
to any measures that could rightly be taken
to succour those in prison and to prevent
needless suffering. The conference met on
the 18th of viii. mo., 1675, and decided that
four times a year representatives from the
various districts should meet in London to
advise as to sufferings which Friends were
undergoing and receive reports which they
might record. It was arranged that the
London representatives should act as a sub-
committee and summon the whole body of
representatives if occasion required, and after
a time the Meeting came to be held monthly
instead of four times a year. Travelling
ministers who might be in London would also
attend its sittings, and other Friends might
be present by invitation. At the present time,
in addition to representatives chosen by each
Quarterly Meeting, any acknowledged minister of the Society and any elder may attend
as of right, and other Friends interested in
any subject under consideration frequently
obtain the leave of the Meeting to be present.

It would hardly be fitting, however, to
conclude this account of the origin of the

organisation of the Society of Friends
without alluding to the remarkable way in
which all their Church meetings and com-
mittees are constituted and arrive at their
decision ; a practice which has remained
unaltered since the earliest days of the
Society. There is in the strictest sense of
the word no chairman at these meetings, but
his place is supplied by the clerk, who usually
has one or more assistants at the table beside
him. It is his duty to bring before the Meeting in order the various subjects which must
be considered, always making room for any
matter of urgency which may arise or for any
subject which a Friend may feel it is his duty
to lay before the Meeting. When a subject
has been considered sufficiently, the clerk
embodies "the sense of the Meeting" in a
draft Minute, which he reads, and corrects,
if necessary, in accordance with the expression of opinion. Under no circumstances
does any vote take place, and the decision
arrived at does not always by any means
represent that of a numerical majority. It is
the duty of the clerk to judge of the value of
opinions expressed, as well as their number,
giving especial heed to the experience and
weight of character of the speakers. In such
discussion oratory is out of place ; there is

no applause, and underlying this disregard of the ordinary methods of a business meeting is the thought of the unseen presence of the Head of the Church, directing all its deliberations. Now and then, although not often, this takes conscious form in the offering of vocal prayer at some occasion of difficulty, or in the solemn pause which sometimes follows as some decision of great importance is reached. The method thus adopted may perhaps be slow, and often results in the temporary postponement of some desired change, in deference to the strong wish of a small minority. But it remains a striking example of the fundamental belief of Quakerism in the reality of the Divine Presence dwelling amongst men and controlling every thought and act of life.

BIBLIOGRAPHICAL NOTE

THE reader will find in the footnotes references to a large number of the principal contemporary sources of information on Quaker history. In addition to these and to other works to which reference has been given, the *Dictionary of National Biography* will be found of great value, especially the article by the Rev. Alexander Gordon on Fox. Use should also be made of the following works :—

Gerard Croese : *Historia Quakeriana.* Amsterdam. 1695. 8vo. (Translated and published in London in 1696 as *The General History of the Quakers.*)
[Inaccurate, and hostile in standpoint, but of considerable interest, especially as having called forth the work of William Sewel, the Quaker Eusebius.]

John Gough : *A History of the People called Quakers.* 4 vols. Dublin. 1789. 8vo.

Samuel M. Janney : *History of the Religious Society of Friends from its rise to the year* 1828. 4 vols. Philadelphia. 1860. 8vo.

Frederick Storrs Turner : *The Quakers. A study Historical and Critical.* London. 1889. 8vo.

A mine of valuable material is contained in the work of Robert Barclay of Tottenham : *The Inner Life of the Religious Societies of the Commonwealth.* London. 1876. 8vo.

Joseph Smith's *Descriptive Catalogue of Friends' Books* (2 vols. London. 1867. 8vo. With *Supplement,* 1893) is an invaluable guide in dealing with early Quaker literature.

The Gresham Press,

UNWIN BROTHERS, LIMITED,

WOKING AND LONDON.